Applications of Computer

An Aid to Professional Undergraduates

The Authors

Dr. Tariq A Raja is working as Professor(Statistics) at Faculty of Veterinary Sciences and Animal husbandry and adjunct faculty at Division of Agri. Statistics, Sher-e- Kashmir University of Agricultural Sciences and Technology-Kashmir (J & K), India. He has passed M.Sc (Statistics) from University of Kashmir, Srinagar (J & K), and has Post Graduation Diploma in Computer Applications and Ph.D (Statistics) from Dr. Bhim Rao Ambedkar University (U.P). He has published one hundred fifteen research papers in various peer reviewed international and national journals and has two manuals and a book to his credit. Besides being in the advisory committee of more than two hundred PG/Ph.D Scholars, Three students have been awarded Ph.D under his guidance. He has presented twenty-five research papers in National and International Conferences. He has organised three training programmes at National level and has received three awards and is executive member of various National and International Societies. At present the author is In-charge Scientist at Central Computer Lab, FVSc & AH, Shuhama SKUAST-Kand can be communicated at tariqaraja@skuastkashmir.ac.in and tariqaraja@rediffmail.com.

Mr. Imtiyaz Ahmad Najar, has been serving as a Computer Programmer (adhoc) in the Central Computer Lab.of Faculty of Veterinary Science & Animal Husbandry for last 8 years. He did his B-Level (MCA) from National Institute of Electronics & Information Technology (NIELIT), New Delhi.He is involved in assignments of imparting Computer Applications in number of courses, in FVSc & AH, besides he has published many Research papers on Computer Applications in National & International journals. He is actively involved in Network Administration in the Faculty and has been appreciated by the officers of University. The author can be mailed at eimtiyazahmad@gmail.com

Applications of Computer

An Aid to Professional Undergraduates

Dr. Tariq Ahmad Raja
Mr. Imtiyaz Ahmad Najar

RAJAT PUBLICATIONS
New Delhi - 110002

APPLICATIONS OF COMPUTER:
AN AID TO PROFESSIONAL UNDERGRADUATES
by Dr. Tariq Ahmad Raja & Mr. Imtiyaz Ahmad Najar

This edition is published by Rajat Publications
4740/23, Ansari Road Daryaganj,
New Delhi - 110002

ISBN: 978-81-7880-838-3

Edition 2025

Printed and bound in India

RAJAT
PUBLICATIONS

4740/23, Ansari Road, Daryaganj,
New Delhi- 110002 (India)
Tel:- +91-11-23267924
Mob:- +91-9811484973, +91-9811105389
E-mail: rajat_publication@yahoo.com

Preface

Computers have brought miraculous changes in the thinking of modern man, like the axe was once considered an extension of human hand. The computers have become extension of human brain. Computers have applications almost in all spheres of life. Its applications are gaining importance in day by day with the development of electronic, communication, information technology and computer industry. It has revolutionized our life-style and education system. Computers play a key role in our everyday lives. In addition to communication media like television, radio and newspaper, we now have another communication medium, i.e. computers. We use computers to e-mail, to chat, for the Internet browsing, for teleconferencing, for video conferencing, etc. We also use them for e-learning, e-commerce, e-banking, e-governance, e-ticketing and for many more things. The interesting part is, while we interact with the other media like television, radio, newspaper, etc. to merely get information, the interaction in computers is two ways—we can act as server as well as a client at other end.

Computer education has become mandatory for every institution. Identifying need of the next generation to be well-equipped to work in ICT. The book is designed in such a way that it not only serves as aguide, but also helps the readers in understanding the fundamentals of computer applications in professional streams.

Computers have been used for statistical processing of data since long. Processing & analysis of data involves, handling data for cross tabulation and carrying out simple to complex computations, which consume considerable amount of time, with the availability of computer, the availability of results are handy. The book explains data analysis using Ms-Excel which gives opportunity to the students to analyze and compute their statistical data.

Starting with an introductory chapter, the book covers topics of computers as well as use of statistical tools in solving the problems. First chapter gives an introduction and overview to computers. This chapter provides an Introduction to Computer Systems, it also discusses about the generation, types, booting, viruses and its management and types of Antivirus programs. Second chapter entitled"Introduction to Operating Systems". discusses about the types of operating system and its features. Chapter three elaborates functioning of "Microsoft Excel 2010" in detail. Chapter four explains mathematical and statistical functions and their use in excel. The various features and functions of data analysis using excel which deals with data analysis tools. Chapter five describes data analysis using MS-Excel which contains correlation, F and T test (parametric tests), and one way and two analysis of variance with illustrations and Non- Parametric tests Wilcoxon Rank Sum Test, Mann-Whitney U Test and Kruskal–Wallis Test, Spearman Rank Correlation Test with illustrations. Chapter Six stresses on graphical features of MS-Excel along with flow charts and algorithm. Chapter seven gives idea about the flow charts for the material in the book with illustrations which will acquaint the end-user with statistical pursuit. Chapter eight provides the information and usage of Database Management System (Microsoft-Access).The last chapter deals with different tools and techniques used in Internet. The book is written in an easy to read style.

The readers are most welcome to bring out and offer valuable suggestions which will be of great help in improving the quality of book.

Tariq A Raja
Imtiyaz A Najar

Contents

Chapter 1

Overview of Computers

Definition

A Computer is a machine which performs calculations and processes data and generates the required output as per the processing instructions given to it.

> *Computer is made up of hardware and software. The computer hardware (machine) is defined in such a way that it does whatever the software (computer programs) tells it to do, so the software acts as a soul to the body.*

The basic operations which a computer performs are.

- **Input:** Inserting or feeding data into the computer by means of an input device like keyboard, joy stick etc.
- **Processing:** Processing is done in the computer to process or transform the data.
- **Output:** A printer or a monitor, Cathode ray tube which shows the result of processing operations.
- **Storage:** The stored result of processing operations for future use is termed as Storage.

These operations are referred to as IPOS cycle.

Five Generations of Computers

Based on the period of development and the features incorporated the computers are classified into different generations.

First Generation (1945-1955)

The first generation computers used vacuum tubes, which made them very bulky and a lot of heat was generated. These Vacuum tube computers are referred to as first generation computers.

1. ENIAC was the first electronic computer which used about 18000 vacuum tubes, 70,000 resistors 5 million soldered joints weighed around 30 tons and occupied the space of a normal house. The operating instructions to the computer were fed externally through different switches and it could do about 300 multiplications task in a second.
2. In 1946 two engineers at the University of Pennsylvania, John Presper Eckert and John W Mauchly invented EDSAC, which became the first computer with the stored program concept. In this computer, there was no need to give instructions externally. Instead, the instructions were stored inside the machine.
3. In 1954 IBM introduced IBM 650 machine which was cheaper than the other alternatives available at that time.

Second Generation (1956-1963)

The transistor greatly changed the computer, transistors, a smaller and more reliable successor were used instead to the vacuum tubes which made them smaller in size and more efficient in computing. These computers generate less heat and were comparatively less expensive in cost.

Third Generation (1964-1971)

Though transistors were clearly an improvement over the vacuum tube, they still generated a great deal of heat which damaged the computers sensitive internal parts, the quartz eliminated this problem. Advances in electronics technology continued and the advent of "microelectronics" technology made it possible to integrate large number of circuit elements into very small (less than 5 mm square) surface of silicon known as "chips". Hundreds of transistors and electronic components were placed on small chips of silicon called ICs (Integrated Circuits). Each IC had a large number of instructions which were built into the chip to perform various operations. The computers designed with this technology were called third generation computers.

Fourth Generation (1971 Onwards)

By integrated circuits the size of computers reduced In the meantime efforts were continued to pack the maximum number of circuits on a single chip. This led to the development of microprocessor on a single chip which contained all the required circuits to do arithmetical, logical and control functions. A fourth generation computers has large scale integration (LSI) chips as its brain. These computers used VLSI (Very Large Scale Integration) technology. It is to the development of LSI/ VLSI technology led to very small but more powerful computers with tremendous speed.

Fifth Generation Computers (Future)

Defining Fifth generation computers are going to use the concept of Artificial Intelligence (A.I) and it can have conversations with the human beings (experts). Artificial intelligence scientists aim to bring us machines with genuine I.Q., the ability to reason logically and with real knowledge of the world. Using Artificial Intelligence, a computer can think and take decisions like a human being after consulting its huge knowledge database. The knowledge database has a very large storage of knowledge with a set of processors which continuously update it.

Input Devices

An input device is any machine that feeds data into a computer. An input device is a device, which accepts data from the outside world, and translates them into a form, which the computer can interpret.

Input data that has previously been recorded on tapes, magnetic tapes, magnetic disks, or floppy disks in a form understood by the program may also be entered into the computer. These are much faster methods than entering data manually form a keyboard.

Several input devices which are available today are mentioned here under:

- Keyboard
- Mouse
- Trackball
- Game controllers
- Joystick
- Digitizing tablet
- Scanner
- Digital camera
- Intelligent character recognition (ICR)
- Magnetic ink character recognition (MICR)
- Optical character recognition (OCR)
- Optical Mark Reader (OMR)
- Barcode Reader
- Voice Recognition
- Light Pen
- Touch Screen and
- Web cams

Output Devices

Output is anything that comes out of a computer. An output device is a device, which accepts data from a computer and translates them into a form, which is suitable for use by the users. In simple words, an output device is any hardware used to communicate the result of data processing carried out by the user or CPU. Output information can be in the form of displayed information or control signals or recordings.

Several output devices include

i) Monitors
ii) CRT Monitor

iii) Flat panel monitor
iv) Liquid Crystal Display (LCD)
v) Thin Film Transistor (TFT)
vi) Light-Emitting Diode (LED)
vii) Printers
viii) Plotters
ix) Screen Image Projector and
x) Voice Response Systems (Speakers).

Memory

Memory is a storing device. It stores programs, data, result, etc. The following are basic two kinds of memory.

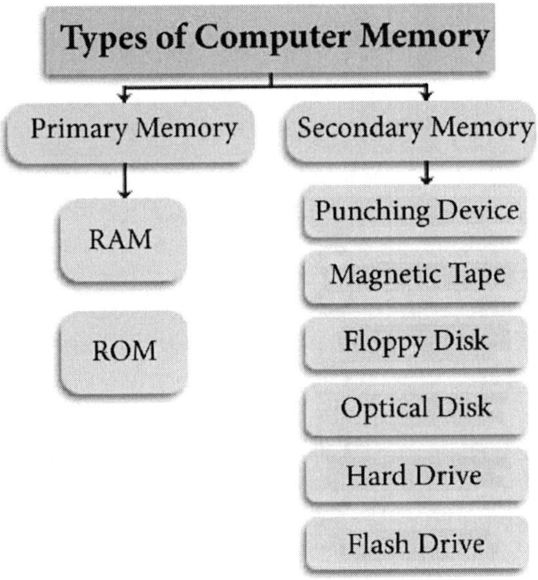

Primary Memory and Secondary Memory

Primary memory is comparatively smaller than that of the secondary memory. Central Processing Unit interacts directly with the primary memory. Random Access Memory (RAM) and Read Only Memory (ROM) ICs are used for main memory. RAMs are volatile in nature, i.e. their contents get erased when power goes off while as ROM is permanent memory.

The *'secondary memory'* is used as huge data storages, and other information like Word Files, Program Files and Games etc. The secondary storage is of a permanent nature, i.e. it stores the information permanently. Magnetic memories like hard disks and floppy disks are commonly used as secondary memories. The classification of memory is done on the basis of primary and secondary memories.

Capacity of Memory

The capacity of memory is measured in bytes. Byte is the smaller unit and means a set of 8 bits.

1 Character = 1 byte = 8 bits
1 Kilo bytes (KB) = 1024 bytes
1 Megabytes (MB) = 1024 KB
1 Giga bytes (GB) = 1024 MB

RAM (Random Access Memory)

Random Access Memory (RAM) is used as a read-write memory of the computer. In RAM, any location can be accessed in a random manner and the access time is the same for each memory location, because the addressing can be done on any location. It is volatile in nature, all data is lost when power is turned off. The RAM is used for temporary storage of programs and fast access.

ROM (Read Only Memory)

Read Only Memory is static, i.e. nothing can be written on it. ROM is a non-volatile memory in nature, i.e. the information stored is not lost when power goes off. The contents of ROM are decided by the hardware manufacturer. The necessary programs are hardwired during the manufacture of computer. It also possesses random access property.

Hardware

Hardware represents the physical components of the computer i.e. The components that can be seen, feel and touched. Input devices, Output devices, CPU, floppy disk, compact disk, flash drives, printers & hard disk etc. are examples of computer hardware.

Software

Set of programs represents Software, which governs the operation of a computer system. Software can be classified broadly into two categories.

1. System Software
2. Application Software

System Software

System software is designed to provide a platform to other software.System software includesoperating systems, computational science software, game engines, industrial automation, and software as service applications.

The system software can further be classified into categories:

- Operating systems.
- Device drivers.
- Middleware.
- Utility software.
- Shells and windowing systems

Application software

Application software is a group of programs designed for end users. It is the set of programs to carry out operations for a specified application. It can further be subdivided into three categories:

i) Packages
ii) Utilities
iii) Customized Software

Packages: Word processing software, spreadsheets, database management systems, desktop publishing software, graphics, multimedia and presentation application.

Utilities: Text Editor, Backup Utility, Compression utility, Disk defragmenter, Antivirus software and **Customized software:** Custom software is software that is specially designed

&developed for some organization or other end user. As such, it can be contrasted with the use of software packages developed for commercial use, or existing free software.

Types of Computer

Computers can be generally classified by size and power as follows, though there is considerable overlap:

- **Personal computer:** A small, single-user computer based on a microprocessor.
- **Workstation:** A powerful, single-user computer. A workstation is like a personal computer, but it has a more powerful microprocessor and, in general, a higher-quality monitor.
- **Minicomputer:** A multi-user computer capable of supporting up to hundreds of users simultaneously
- **Mainframe:** A powerful multi-user computer capable of supporting many hundreds or thousands of users simultaneously.
- **Supercomputer:** An extremely fast computer that can perform hundreds of millions of instructions per second.

Personal Computer

Computer designed for an individual. These computers start from few thousand bucks. All are based on the microprocessor technology that enables manufacturers to put an entire CPU on one chip. Businesses use personal computers for word processing, accounting, desktop publishing, and for running spreadsheet and database management applications. At home, the most popular use for personal computers is for playing games and recently for surfing the Internet.

Personal computers first appeared in the late 1970s. One of the first and most popular personal computers was the Apple II, introduced in 1977 by Apple Computer. During the late 1970s and early 1980s, new models and competing operating systems seemed to appear daily. Then, in 1981, IBM entered the fray with its first personal computer, known as the IBM PC. The IBM PC quickly became the personal computer of choice, and most other personal computer manufacturers fell by the wayside. P.C. is short for personal computer or IBM PC. One of the few companies to survive IBM's onslaught was Apple Computer, which remains a major player in the personal computer marketplace. Other companies adjusted to IBM's dominance by building IBM clones, computers that were internally almost the same as the IBM PC, but that cost less. Because IBM clones used the same microprocessors as IBM PCs, they were capable of running the same software. Over the years, IBM has lost much of its influence in directing the evolution of PCs. Therefore after the release of the first PC by IBM the term PC increasingly came to mean IBM or IBM-compatible personal computers, to the exclusion of other types of personal computers, such as Macintoshes. In recent years, the term PC has become more and more difficult to pin down. In general, though, it applies to any personal computer based on an Intel microprocessor, or on an Intel-compatible microprocessor. For nearly every other component, including the operating system, there are several options, all of which fall under the book of PC.

Today, the world of personal computers is basically divided between Apple Macintoshes and PCs. The principal characteristics of personal computers are that they are single-user systems and are based on microprocessors. However, although personal computers are designed as single-user systems, it is common to link them together to form a network. In terms of power, there is great variety. At the high end, the distinction between personal computers and workstations has faded. High-end models of the Macintosh and PC offer the same computing power and graphics capability as low-end workstations by Sun Microsystems, Hewlett-Packard, and DEC.

Personal Computer Types

Personal computers can be generally classified by size and chassis / case. The chassis or case is the metal frame that serves as the structural support for electronic components. Every computer system requires at least one chassis to house the circuit boards and wiring. The chassis also contains slots for expansion boards. If you want to insert more boards than there are slots, you will need an expansion chassis, which provides additional slots. There are two basic flavors of chassis designs–desktop models and tower models–but there are many variations on these two basic types. Then come the portable computers that are computers small enough to carry. Portable computers include notebook and subnotebook computers, hand-held computers, palmtops, and PDAs.

Desktop Model

A desktop computer is a personal computer designed for regular use at a single location on or near a desk or table due to its size and power requirements. The most common configuration has a case that houses the power supply, motherboard (a printed circuit board with a microprocessor as the central processing unit (CPU), memory, bus, and other electronic components), disk storage (usually one or more hard disk drives, optical disc drives, and in early models a floppy disk drive); a keyboard and mouse for input; and a computer monitor, speakers, and, often, a printer for output. The case may be oriented horizontally or vertically and placed either underneath, beside, or on top of a desk.

Notebook Computer

An extremely lightweight personal computer. Notebook computers typically weigh less than 6 pounds and are small enough to fit easily in a briefcase. Aside from size, the principal difference between a notebook computer and a personal computer is the display screen. Notebook computers use a variety of techniques, known as flat-panel technologies, to produce a lightweight and non-bulky display screen. In terms of computing power, modern notebook computers are nearly equivalent to personal computers. They have the same CPUs, memory capacity, and disk drives.

Laptop Computer

A small, portable computer small enough that it can sit on your lap. Nowadays, laptop computers are more frequently called notebook computers.

Subnotebook Computer

A portable computer that is slightly lighter and smaller than a full-sized notebook computer. Typically, subnotebook computers have a smaller keyboard and screen, but are otherwise equivalent to notebook computers.

Hand-held Computer

A portable computer that is small enough to be held in one's hand. Although extremely convenient to carry, handheld computers have not replaced notebook computers because of their small keyboards and screens. The most popular hand-held computers are those that are specifically designed to provide PIM (personal information manager) functions, such as a calendar and address book. Some manufacturers are trying to solve the small keyboard problem by replacing the keyboard with an electronic pen. However, these pen-based devices rely on handwriting recognition technologies, which are still in their infancy. Hand-held computers are also called PDAs, Palmtops and Pocket computers.

Palmtop

A small computer that literally fits in your palm. Compared to full-size computers, palmtops are severely limited, but they are practical for certain functions such as phone books and calendars. Palmtops that use a pen rather than a keyboard for input are often called hand-held computers or PDAs. Because of their small size, most palmtop computers do not include disk drives. However, many contain PCMCIA slots in which you can insert disk drives, modems, memory, and other devices.

PDA

Short for personal digital assistant, a handheld device that combines computing, telephone/fax, and networking features. A typical PDA can function as a cellular phone, fax sender, and personal organizer. Unlike portable computers, most PDAs are pen-based, using a stylus rather than a keyboard for input. This means that they also incorporate handwriting recognition features. Some PDAs can also react to voice input by using voice recognition technologies. The field of PDA was pioneered by Apple Computer, which introduced the Newton Message Pad in 1993. Shortly thereafter, several other manufacturers offered similar products. To date, PDAs have had only modest success in the marketplace, due to their high price tags and limited applications. However, many experts believe that PDAs will eventually become common gadgets.

PDAs are also called palmtops, hand-held computers and pocket computers.

Workstation

A workstation is a computer intended for engineering use that is faster and more capable than a personal computer. It's intended for business or professional use (rather than home or recreational use). Workstations and applications designed for them are used by small engineering companies, architects, graphic designers, and any organization, department, or individual that requires a faster microprocessor, a large amount of random access memory (RAM), and special features such as high-speed graphics adapters. Historically, the workstation developed technologically about the same time and for the same audience as the UNIX operating system, which is often used as the workstation operating system. Among the most successful makers of this kind of workstation are Sun Microsystems, Hewlett-Packard, DEC, and IBM

Minicomputer

A minicomputer is a type of computer that possesses most of the features and capabilities of a large computer but is smaller in physical size.

A minicomputer fills the space between the mainframe and microcomputer, and is smaller than the mainframe but larger than the microcomputer. Minicomputers are mainly used as small or mid-range servers, operating business and scientific applications. However, the use of the term minicomputer has diminished and has merged with servers. It is mostly used in multiprocessing environment.

Mainframe

Mainframe was a term originally referring to the cabinet containing the central processor unit or "main frame" of a room-filling Stone Age batch machine. After the emergence of smaller "minicomputer" designs in the early 1970s, the traditional big iron machines were described as "mainframe computers" and eventually just as mainframes. Mainframe is a very large and expensive computer capable of supporting hundreds, or even thousands, of users simultaneously. The main difference between a supercomputer and a mainframe is that a supercomputer channels all its power into executing a few programs as fast as possible, whereas a mainframe uses its power to execute many programs concurrently. In some ways, mainframes are more powerful than supercomputers because they support more simultaneous programs. But supercomputers can execute a single program faster than a mainframe. Mainframe computers are computers used primarily by large organizations for critical applications; bulk data processing, such as census, industry and consumer statistics, enterprise resource planning; and transaction processing.

Supercomputer

A supercomputer is the fastest computer in the world that can process a significant amount of data very quickly. The computing performance of a "supercomputer" is measured very high as compared to a general purpose computer. The computing performance of a supercomputer is measured in FLOPS (that is floating-point operations per second) instead of MIPS. The supercomputer consists of tens of thousands of processors which can perform billions and trillions of calculations per second, or you can say that supercomputers can deliver up to nearly a hundred quadrillions of FLOPS. They have evolved from grid to cluster system of massively parallel computing. Cluster system computing means that machine uses multiple processors in one system instead of arrays of separate computers in a network. These computers are most massive concerning size. A most powerful supercomputer can occupy few feet to hundreds of feet. The supercomputer price is very high, and they can vary from 2 lakh dollar to over 100 million dollars. Supercomputers were introduced in the 1960s and developed by Seymour Cray with the Atlas at the University of Manchester. The Cray designed CDC 1604 which was the first supercomputer in the world.

Booting

Booting is a start-up sequence that starts the operating system of a computer when it is turned on. A boot sequence is the initial set of operations that the computer performs when it is switched on. Every computer has a boot sequence. The average computer doesn't understand the boot sequence but is important to know for customizing and troubleshooting your computer.

Boot Loader

Computers powered by the central processing unit can only execute code found in the systems memory. Modern operating systems, applications, program code and data are stored on non-volatile memories or mass storage devices. When a computer is first powered on, it must initially rely only on the code and data stored in non-volatile portions of the systems memory. At boot time, the operating system is not really loaded and the computer's hardware cannot perform many complex systems actions.

The program that starts the "chain reaction" which ends with the entire operating system being loaded is known as the boot loader (or bootstrap loader). The term creatively came from early designers imagining that before a computer "runs" it must have it is "boots strapped". The boot loader's only job is to load other software for the operating system to start. Often, multiple-stage boot loaders are used, in which several small programs of increasing complexity sequentially summon one after the other, until the last of them loads the operating system.

Boot Devices

The boot device is the device from which the operating system is loaded. A modern PC BIOS (Basic Input/Output System) supports booting from various devices. These include the local hard disk drive, optical drive, floppy drive, a network interface card, and a USB device. Typically, the BIOS will allow the user to configure a boot order. If the boot order is set to:

1. CD Drive
2. Hard Disk Drive
3. Network

After selecting the appropriate Boot device the BIOS will try to boot from the CD drive first, and if that fails then it will try to boot from the hard disk drive, and if that fails then it will try to boot from the network, and if that fails then it won't boot at all.

Boot Sequence

There is a standard boot sequence that all personal computers use. First, the CPU runs an instruction in memory for the BIOS. That instruction contains a jump instruction that transfers to the BIOS start-up program. This program runs a power-on self-test (POST) to check that devices the computer will rely on are functioning properly. Then, the BIOS goes through the configured boot sequence until it finds a device that is bootable. Once BIOS has found a bootable device, BIOS loads the boot sector and transfers execution to the boot sector. If the boot device is a hard drive, it will be a master boot record (MBR). The MBR code checks the partition table for an active partition. If one is found the MBR code loads that partition's boot sector and executes it. The boot sector is often operating system specific, however in most operating systems its main function is to load and execute the operating system kernel, which continues start up. If there is no active partition or the active partition's boot sector is invalid, the MBR may load a secondary boot loader which will select a partition and load its boot bootsector, which usually loads the corresponding operating system kernel.

Virus

The computer virus is a program that can create havoc or just be a general nuisance on a computer. Some are malicious, while others can be annoyingly humorous. Viruses show us how vulnerable we are, a properly engineered virus can have a devastating effect, disrupting productivity and doing damage.

Viruses can increase their chance of spreading to other computers by infecting files.

There are many different forms of electronic infection. The most common are:

- **Viruses:** In general, it is a small malicious program that piggybacks on real programs. For example, a virus, such as an executable or macro might attach itself to a program such as a spreadsheet program. Each time the spreadsheet program runs, the virus runs too allowing it to replicate by attaching to other programs or create havoc.
- **E-mail viruses:** An e-mail virus travels as an attachment through e-mail messages, and usually replicates itself by automatically mailing itself to contacts in the victim's e-mail address book. Some e-mail viruses don't even require a double-click they launch when you view the infected message in the preview pane of your e-mail software.
- **Trojan horses:** A Trojan horse is simply a computer program. The program claims to do one thing, such as game you download, but instead does damage when you run it. Trojan horses have no way to replicate automatically.
- **Worms:** A worm is a small piece of software that uses computer networks and security holes to replicate itself. A copy of the worm scans the network for another machine that has a specific security hole. It copies itself to the new machine using the security hole, and then starts replicating from there, as well.

Virus Origins

Computer viruses are much like biological viruses. A computer virus passes from computer to computer like a biological virus passes from person to person. Unlike a human virus, a computer virus has no way to reproduce by itself.

A computer virus acts in a similar way. A computer virus must piggyback on top of some other program or document in order to launch. Once the virus runs, it can infect other programs or documents. A computer can only catch a virus if it comes in contact with another infected computer through e-mail, sharing of disks, CD's, flash drives or the internet file sharing programs.

Viruses do not just appear by themselves. People write computer viruses. A person has to write the code, test it to make sure it spreads properly and then release it. A person also designs the virus's attack phase, whether it's a silly message or the destruction of a hard disk. Why do they do it?

There are at least three reasons. The first reason is psychological. Why would someone want to break a window on someone's car, paint signs on buildings or burn down a beautiful forest? If that sort of person knows computer programming, then he or she may funnel energy into the creation of destructive viruses.

The second reason has to do with the thrill. Some people have a fascination with things like explosions and car wrecks. When you were growing up, there might have been a kid in your neighborhood who learned how to make gunpowder. That kid probably built bigger and bigger bombs until he either got bored or did some serious damage. Creating a virus is a little like that it creates a bomb inside a computer, and the more computers that get infected the more "fun" the explosion.

The third reason is to get some "street cred", bragging rights for accomplishing such a feat. Think of Mount Everest -- the mountain is there, so someone climbs it. If you are a certain type of programmer who sees a security hole that could be breached, you might be compelled to "break in" before someone else does.

Most virus creators are just punks who miss the point that they cause real damage to real people with their creations. Destroying everything on a person's hard disk is real damage. Forcing a large company to waste thousands of hours cleaning up after a virus is real damage. Even a silly message is real damage because someone has to spend time getting rid of it. For these reasons, the law is getting much harsher in punishing the people who create viruses.

Virus History

Computer viruses first appeared in the late 1980's with the spread of personal computers. Prior to the 1980's, home computers were nearly non-existent or they were toys. Computers started to spread with the popularity of the IBM PC (released in 1982) and the Apple Macintosh (released in 1984). The second factor was the use of computer bulletin boards that people would access through a modem and download programs of all types. Games were extremely popular as were simple word processor, spreadsheets and other software. This led to the precursor of the virus known as the Trojan horse, a program downloaded by a user not knowing it was an actual virus. The third factor that led to the creation of viruses was the floppy disk. Programs were small enough to fit the entire operating system, a few programs and some documents onto a floppy disk. Many computers did not have hard disks, so when you turned on your machine it would load the operating system and everything else from the floppy disk. Virus authors took advantage of this to create the first self-replicating programs.

Early viruses were pieces of code attached to a common program like a popular game or a popular word processor. A person might download an infected game from a bulletin board and run it.

This small piece of code embedded in a larger, legitimate program. When the user ran the legitimate program, the virus loaded itself into memory¬ and added itself into program code. If an infected program was given to another person on a floppy disk or was uploaded to a bulletin board, then other programs got infected. This was how the early virus spread.

The spreading part is the infection phase of the virus. Viruses wouldn't be despised if all they did was replicate. Most viruses also have a destructive attack phase where they do damage. Some sort of trigger will activate the attack phase and the virus will then launch. The two main functions of a virus are to replicate and activate.

Virus Evolution

As virus creators became more sophisticated, they learned new tricks. One important trick was the ability to load viruses into memory so they could keep running in the background as long as the computer remained on. This gave viruses a much more effective way to replicate themselves. Another trick was the ability to infect the boot sector on floppy disks and hard disks. The boot sector is a small program that is the first part of the operating system that the computer loads. It contains a tiny program that tells the computer how to start up. By putting its code in the boot sector, a virus can guarantee it is executed. It can load itself into memory immediately and run whenever the computer is on. Boot sector viruses infected the boot sector of any floppy disk inserted in the machine, and on college campuses, where lots of people shared machines, they could spread like wildfire.

In general, neither executable nor boot sector viruses are very threatening any longer. The first reason for the decline has been the amount of disk space programs now require. Nearly every new program comes on a CD. Compact discs (CDs) cannot be modified making viral infection by a CD unlikely, unless the manufacturer mistakenly placed a virus onto the CD during production. The programs are so big that the only easy way to move them around is to buy the CD. People certainly can't carry applications around on floppy disks like they did in the 1980s, when floppies full of programs were traded like baseball cards. Boot sector viruses have also declined because operating systems now protect the boot sector.

Infection from boot sector viruses and executable viruses is still possible. It is a lot harder and these viruses don't spread as quickly as they once did. Call it "shrinking habitat," if you want to use a biological analogy. The environment of floppy disks, small programs and weak operating systems made these viruses possible in the 1980s, but that environmental has been largely eliminated by huge files, unchangeable CDs and better operating system safeguards.

E-mail Viruses

Virus authors adapted to the changes in technology by creating the e-mail virus. For example, the Melissa virus in March 1999 spread in Microsoft Word documents sent via e-mail. The ILOVEYOU virus, which appeared on May 4, 2000, contained a piece of code as an attachment. These were more of a Trojan horse distributed by e-mail.

Worms

A worm is a computer program that has the ability to copy itself from machine to machine. Worms use up computer time and network bandwidth when they replicate, and often carry payloads that do considerable damage.

A worm usually exploits a security hole in a piece of software or the operating system. Worms normally move around and infect other machines through computer networks. Using a network, a worm can multiply from a single copy quickly. A worm called Code Red made huge headlines in 2001. Experts predicted that this worm could clog the Internet so effectively that things would completely grind to a halt. The Code Red worm replicated itself more than 250,000 times in approximately nine hours on July 19, 2001.

When the worm is launched, it opens a back door into the computer, adds the infected machine to a botnet and installs code that hides itself. Like most viruses, it operates in a stealth mode to avoid detection. The botnets are small peer-to- peer groups rather than a larger, more easily identified network. Experts think the people controlling Storm rent out their micro-botnets to deliver spam or adware or for denial-of-service attacks on Web sites.

Measure to Protect Computer from Viruses

Computers can be protected against viruses by specialized Antivirus programs.

Antivirus Software

Antivirus software, originally designed to detect and remove viruses from computers, can also protect against a wide variety of threats, including other types of malicious software, such as key-loggers, browser hijackers, Trojan horses, worms, rootkits, spyware, adware, botnets and ransomware.

How Antivirus Software Works

Antivirus software typically runs as a background process, scanning computers, servers or mobile devices to detect and restrict the spread of malware. Many antivirus software programs include real-time threat detection and protection to guard against potential vulnerabilities as they happen, as well as system scans that monitor device and system files looking for possible risks.

Antivirus software usually performs these basic functions:

- Scanning directories or specific files for known malicious patterns indicating the presence of malicious software;
- Allowing users to schedule scans so they run automatically allowing users to initiate new scans at any time and removing any malicious software it detects. Some antivirus software programs do this automatically in the background, while others notify users of infections and ask them if they want to clean the files.

In order to scan systems comprehensively, antivirus software must generally be given privileged access to the entire system. This makes antivirus software itself a common target for attackers, and researchers have discovered remote code execution and other serious vulnerabilities in antivirus software products in recent years.

Types of Antivirus Programs

Antivirus software is distributed in a number of forms, including stand-alone antivirus scanners and internet security suites that offer antivirus protection, along with firewalls, privacy controls and other security protections.

Some antivirus software vendors offer basic versions of their products at no charge. These free versions generally offer basic antivirus and spyware protection, but more advanced features and protections are usually available only to subscribers.

While some operating systems are targeted more frequently by virus developers, antivirus software is available for most Operating Systems:

- Windows antivirus software. Most antivirus software vendors offer several levels of Windows products at different price points, starting with free versions offering only basic protection. Users must start scans and updates manually and typically free versions of antivirus software won't protect against links to malicious websites or malicious attachments in emails. Premium versions of antivirus software often include suites of endpoint security tools that may provide secure online storage, ad blockers and file encryption. Since 2004, Microsoft has been offering some kind of free antivirus software as part of the Windows operating system itself, generally under the name Windows Defender, though the software was mostly limited to detecting spyware prior to 2006.
- MacOS antivirus software. Although macOS viruses exist, they're less common than Windows viruses, so antivirus products for macOS are less standardized than those for Windows. There are a number of free and paid products available, providing on-demand tools to protect against potential malware threats through full-system malware scans and the ability to scrutinize through specific email threads, attachments and various web activities.
- Android antivirus software. Android is the world's most popular mobile operating system and is installed on more mobile devices than any other OS. Because most mobile malware targets Android, experts recommend all Android device users install antivirus software on their devices. Vendors offer a variety of basic free and paid premium versions of their Android antivirus software including anti-theft and remote-locating features. Some run automatic scans and actively try to stop malicious web pages and files from being opened or downloaded.

Chapter 2

Introduction to Operating Systems

An operating system (OS), in its most general sense, is software that allows a user to run other applications on a computing device. While it is possible for a software application to interface directly with hardware, the vast majority of applications are written for an OS, which allows them to take advantage of common libraries and not worry about specific hardware details.

The OS also provides services to facilitate the efficient execution and management of, and memory allocations for, any additional installed software application programs.

An operating system performs these services for applications:

- In a multitasking operating system where multiple programs can be running at the same time, the operating system determines which applications should run in what order and how much time should be allowed for each application before giving another application a turn.
- It manages the sharing of internal memory among multiple applications.
- It handles input and output to and from attached hardware devices, such as hard disks, printers, and dial-up ports.

- It sends messages to each application or interactive user (or to a system operator) about the status of operation and any errors that may have occurred.
- It can off load the management of what are called batch jobs (for example, printing) so that the initiating application is freed from this work.
- On computers that can provide parallel processing, an operating system can manage how to divide the program so that it runs on more than one processor at a time.
- All major computer platforms (hardware and software) require and sometimes include an operating system, and operating systems must be developed with different features to meet the specific needs of various form factors.

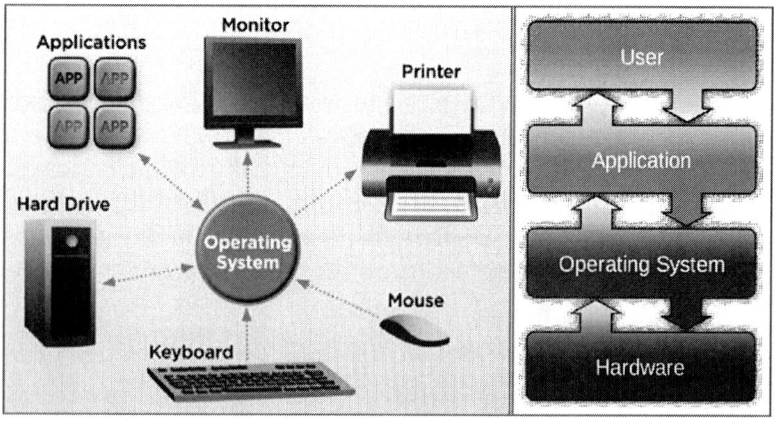

The need for the Operating System arises from the fact that user needs to be provided with services and OS facilitates the provisioning of these services. User application would need to store information. The OS makes memory available to an application when required. Similarly, user applications need use of input facility to communicate with the application. This is often in the form of a key board, or a mouse or even a joy stick (if the application is a game for instance). The output usually provided by a video monitor or a printer as some times the user may wish to generate an output in the form of a printed document. Output may be available in some other forms. For example it may be a video or an audio file.

Let us consider few applications.

- Image processing (Graphics)
- Auto CAD
- E-mail
- Accounting
- Document Design
- Games

We notice that each of the above application requires resources for

- Storage of information
- Processing information
- Output Devices
- Input Devices

The OS offers services to support all the above operations. These operations in turn facilitate the applications mentioned earlier. To that extent an OS operation is application neutral and service specific.

Functions of Operating System

The operating system sets the standards for all application programs that run in the computer. Also called an 'executive' or 'supervisor', an operating system performs the following functions:

1. *User Interface.* The user interface includes the windows, menus and method of interaction between users and the computer.
2. *Job Management. Job management controls the order and time in which programs are run and is more sophisticated in the mainframe environment where scheduling the daily work has always been routine.*
3. *Task Management. Multitasking, which is the ability to simultaneously* execute multiple programs, is now available in all operating systems. Critical in the

mainframe and server environment, applications can be prioritized to run faster or slower depending on their purpose.

4. *Data Management.* Data management keeps track of the data storage devices. The operating system's file system knows where that data are physically stored.
5. *Device Management.* Device management controls peripheral devices by sending those commands in their own proprietary language. The OS requires drivers for the peripherals attached to the computer. When a new peripheral is added, that device's driver is installed into operating system.
6. *Security.* Operating systems such as Windows 2000 provide password protection to keep unauthorized users out of the system. Some operating systems also provide backup and recovery routines for starting over in the event of a system failure.
7. *Networking.* Most current operating systems are capable of using the TCP/IP networking protocols. This means that one system can appear on a network of the other and share resources such as files, printers, and scanners, using either wired or wireless connections.

Types of Operating System

Operating systems usually come pre-loaded on any computer you buy. Most people use the operating system that comes with their computer, but it's possible to upgrade or even change operating systems. The three most common operating systems for personal computers are Microsoft Windows, Mac OS X and Linux. Modern operating systems use a graphical user interface, or GUI (pronounced gooey). A GUI lets you use your mouse to click icons, buttons, and menus, and everything is clearly displayed on the screen using a combination of graphics and text. Each operating system's GUI has a different look and feel, so if you switch to a different operating system it may seem unfamiliar at first. However, modern operating systems are designed to be easy to use, and most of the basic principles are the same.

Microsoft Windows

Microsoft created the Windows operating system in the mid-1980s. Over the years, there have been many different versions of Windows, but the most recent ones are Windows 10 (released in 2015), Windows 8 (2012), Windows 7 (2009), and Windows Vista (2007). Windows comes pre-loaded on most new PCs, which helps to make it the most popular operating system in the world.

Mac OS

Mac OS is a line of operating systems created by Apple. It comes preloaded on all new Macintosh computers, or Macs. All of the recent versions are known as OS X (pronounced O-S Ten), and the specific versions include El Capitan (released in 2015), Yosemite (2014), Mavericks (2013), Mountain Lion (2012), and Lion (2011).

According to Stat Counter Global Stats, Mac OS X users account for less than 10% of global operating systems—much lower than the percentage of Windows users (more than 80%). One reason for this is that Apple computers tend to be more expensive. However, many people do prefer the look and feel of Mac OS X over Windows.

Linux

Linux (pronounced LINN-ux) is a family of open-source operating systems, which means they can be modified and distributed by anyone around the world. This is different from proprietary *software* like Windows, which can only be modified by the company that owns it. The advantages of Linux are that it is *free*, and there are many different *distributions*—or versions—you can choose from.

According to Stat Counter Global Stats, Linux users account for less than 2% of global operating systems. However, most *servers* run Linux because it's relatively easy to customize.

Operating Systems for Mobile Devices

The operating systems we've been talking about so far were designed to run on *desktop* and *laptop* computers. *Mobile devices* such as *phones, tablet computers,* and *MP3 players* are different from desktop and laptop computers, so they run operating systems that are designed specifically for mobile devices. Examples of mobile operating systems include *Apple iOS* and *Google Android*. In the screenshot below, you can see iOS running on an iPad.

Operating systems for mobile devices generally aren't as fully featured as those made for desktop and laptop computers, and they aren't able to run all of the same software. However, you can still do a lot of things with them, like watch movies, browse the Web, manage your calendar, and play games.

MS-DOS

Short for Microsoft Disk Operating System, MS-DOS is a non-graphical command line operating system derived from 86-DOS that was created for IBM compatible computers. MS-DOS originally written by Tim Paterson and introduced by Microsoft in August 1981 and was last updated in 1994 when MS-DOS 6.22 was released. MS-DOS allows the user to navigate, open, and otherwise manipulate files on their computer from a command line instead of a GUI like Windows.

MS-DOS is no longer used; however, the command shell, more commonly known as the Windows command line is still used by many users.

Main features of MS-DOS are as follows:

1. *User Interface.* MS-DOS employs a command line interface and a batch scripting facility via its command interpreter, COMMAND.COM.
2. *Multitasking.* MS-DOS was not designed to be a multi-user or multitasking operating system, but many attempts were made to add these capabilities.

How do you communicate with DOS?

The original DOS was an entirely text based system. All it provided for the user was a command prompt: "C:>" or "A:>", where the user would type in commands from the keyboard. The system was entirely case insensitive: so either "ForMAt C:" or "format c:" would erase your hard disk.

The latter example is of course a small warning: with DOS or OS comes power, you can very easily mess up your system if you use powerful commands in the wrong way. The commands you should be careful of are: "Format", "Recover", and "Del". All of these perform useful functions, when used correctly, and all the others are pretty much safe to use.

All modern Operating Systems including Windows continue to use, and have available some form of the command prompt (C:\>). There are times when it is easier or quicker to issue a text-based command then to open and use a graphical-based window, especially when the response to a command is a single word or phrase or only text-based information.

How is DOS used?

When you type anything at the DOS prompt, and press enter, you are telling DOS to run a program.

It will first look to see if there is an internal command program which has that name, and if it does not find one, then it will look to see if there is a file on disk with that name.

If it finds an external file with the extension .COM (command), or .EXE (executable), then the program is loaded and run. At this point DOS loses control of the computer until the program has ended. However parts of it are still used by the programs as they are running, eg to load and save files etc.

Useful internal DOS commands:

- A: - Change current directory path to the floppy disk drive
- C: - Change current directory path to the hard disk drive
- DIR - Display current directory (show all files and sub-directories).
- MD - Make a new directory, eg: MD C:\EMAIL
- CD - Change current directory, eg. CD C:\EMAIL
- COPY - Copy file(s) from one place to another.
- Del - Delete/erase a file

Any other text on the input line after the file name, is passed to the program. This means that in the command "Copy help.txt help.bak", the text, "help.txt and help.bak" is passed to the copy program which will in this case use it to specify source and destination files for a copy.

DOS usage examples:

DIR [enter]
Displays the current directory listing.

DIR *.txt [enter]
Displays any files in the current directory with .TXT as their extension

DIR A:\PICTURES[enter]
Displays a directory listing for the path, A:\PICTURES

A: [enter]
MD PICTURES [enter]
CD PICTURES [enter]

DIR
Change to the floppy disk drive A:, make a directory called PICTURES, change the current directory to PICTURES, and then list (display) all the contents (files and subdirectories) in the directory PICTURES.

COPY letter.txt letter.bak [enter]
Copy the file "letter.txt" to a file called "letter.bak". (Creates "letter.bak" if it does not exist, and overwrites it if it does).

COPY A:\pictures*.pic C:\ [enter]
Copy any file with an extension PIC from the A: floppy drive, in the PICTURES directory to the root directory of the hard disk.

Chapter 3

Microsoft-Excel (Ms-Excel 2010)

The following basic window appears when you start the excel application. Let us now understand the various important parts of this window.

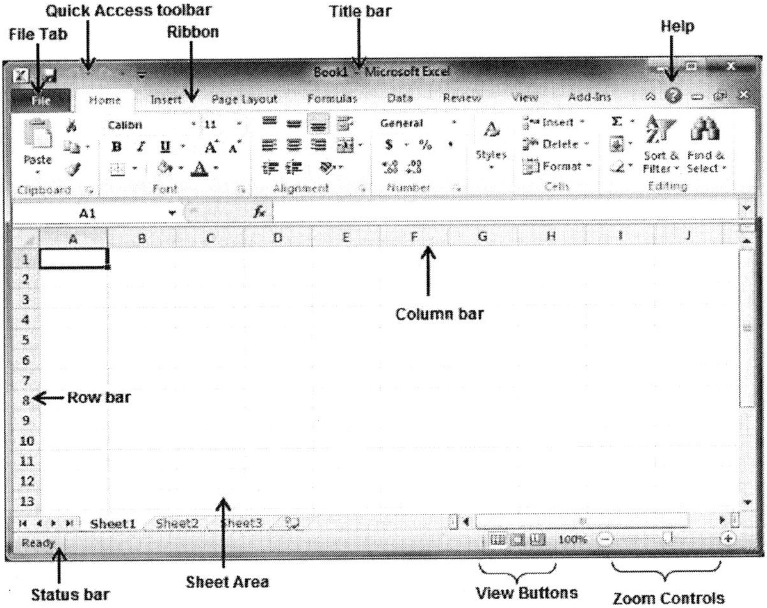

File Tab

The File tab replaces the Office button from Excel 2007. You can click it to check the back stage view, where you come to open or save files, create new sheets, print a sheet, and do other file-related operations.

Quick Access Toolbar

You will find this toolbar just above the File tab and its purpose is to provide a convenient resting place for the Excel's most frequently used commands. You can customize this toolbar based on your comfort.

Ribbon

Ribbon contains commands organized in three components:

Tabs

They appear across the top of the Ribbon and contain groups of related commands. Homes, Insert, Page Layout are the examples of ribbon tabs.

Groups

They organize related commands; each group name appears below the group on the Ribbon. For example, group of commands related to fonts or group of commands related to alignment etc.

Commands

Commands appear within each group as mentioned above.

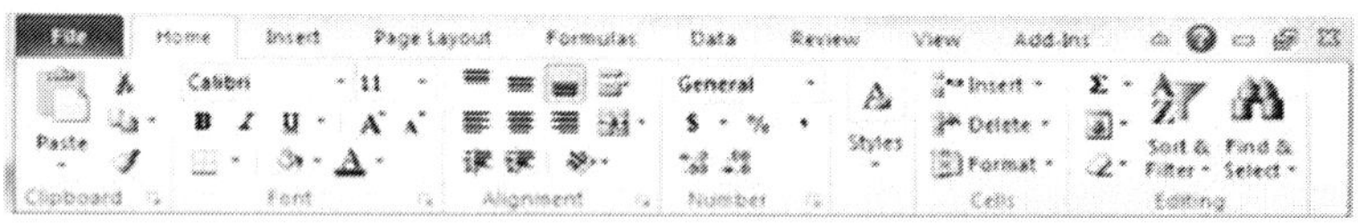

Title Bar

This lies in the middle and at the top of the window. Title bar shows the program and the sheet titles.

Help

The Help Icon can be used to get excel related help anytime you like. This provides nice tutorial on various subjects related to excel.

Zoom Control

Zoom control lets you zoom in for a closer look at your text. The zoom control consists of a slider that you can slide left or right to zoom in or out. The + buttons can be clicked to increase or decrease the zoom factor.

View Buttons

The group of three buttons located to the left of the Zoom control, near the bottom of the screen, lets you switch among Excel's has various sheet views, as mentioned below.

- *Normal Layout view:* This displays the page in normal view.
- *Page Layout view:* This displays pages exactly as they will appear when printed. This gives a full screen look of the document.
- *Page Break view:* This shows a preview of where pages will break when printed.

Sheet Area

The area where you enter data. The flashing vertical bar is called the insertion point and it represents the location where text will appear when you type.

Row Bar

Rows are numbered from 1 onwards and keep on increasing as you keep entering data. Maximum limit is 1,048,576 rows.

Column Bar

Columns are numbered from A onwards and keeps on increasing as you keep entering data. After Z, it will start the series of AA, AB and so on. Maximum limit is 16,384 columns.

Status Bar

This displays the sheet information as well as the insertion point location. From left to right, this bar can contain the total number of pages and words in the document, language etc. You can configure the status bar by right-clicking anywhere on it and by selecting or deselecting options from the provided list.

Dialog Box Launcher:

This appears as a very small arrow in the lower-right corner of many groups on the Ribbon. Clicking this button opens a dialog box or task pane that provides more options about the group

Backstage View

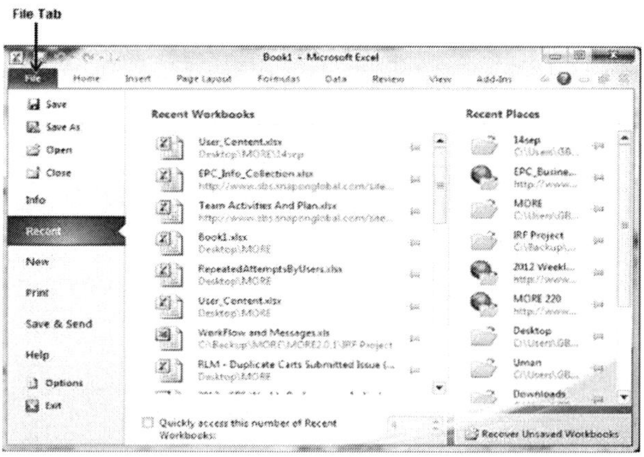

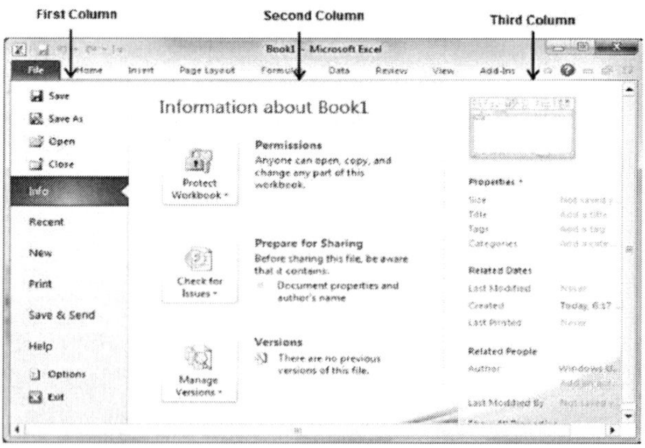

The Backstage view has been introduced in Excel 2010 and acts as the central place for managing your sheets. The backstage view helps in creating new sheets, saving and opening sheets, printing and sharing sheets, and so on. Getting to the Backstage View is easy. Just click the File tab located in the upper-left corner of the Excel Ribbon. If you already do not have any opened sheet then you will see a window listing down all the recently opened sheets as follows:

If you already have an opened sheet then it will display a window showing the details about the opened sheet as shown below. Backstage view shows three columns when you select most of the available options in the first column. First column of the backstage view will have the following options:

Option	Description
Save	If an existing sheet is opened, it would be saved as it is; otherwise it will display a dialogue box asking for the sheet name.
Save As	A dialogue box will be displayed asking for sheet name and sheet type. By default, it will save in sheet 2010 Format with extension .xlsx.
Open	This option is used to open an existing excel sheet.
Close	This option is used to close an opened sheet.
Info	This option displays the information about the opened sheet.
Recent	This option lists down all the recently opened sheets.
New	New This option is used to open a new sheet.
Print	Print This option is used to print an opened sheet.
Save & Send	This option saves an opened sheet and displays options to send the sheet using email etc.
Help	You can use this option to get the required help about excel 2010.
Options	Use this option to set various option related to excel 2010.
Exit	Use this option to close the sheet and exit.

Entering Values in Excel Sheet

Entering values in excel sheet is a easy task and this chapter shows how to enter values in an excel sheet. A new sheet is displayed by default when you open an excel sheet as shown in the below screen shot Sheet area is the place where you type your text. The flashing vertical bar is called the insertion point and it represents the location where text will appear when you type. When you click on a box then the box is highlighted. When you double click the box, the flashing vertical bar appears and you can start entering your data. So, just keep your mouse cursor at the text insertion point and start typing whatever text you would like to type. We have typed only two words "Hello Excel" as shown below. The text appears to the left of the insertion point as you type

There are following three important points, which would help you while typing:

Press Tab to go to next column.

Press Enter to go to next row.

Press Alt + Enter to enter a new line in the same column.

Excel provides a number of ways to move around a sheet using the mouse and the keyboard.

First of all, let us create some sample text before we proceed. Open a new excel sheet and type any data. We've shown a sample data in the screen shot.

Order Date	Name	Item	Units	Cost	Total Cost
1/6/2017	Tariq	Pencil	95	1.99	189.05
1/23/2017	Zaffar	Binder	50	19.99	999.5
2/26/2017	Athar	Pen	27	19.99	539.73
3/15/2017	Faheem	Pencil	56	2.99	167.44
4/1/2017	Imtiyaz	Binder	60	4.99	299.4
4/18/2017	Zahoor	Pencil	75	1.99	149.25

Moving with Mouse

You can easily move the insertion point by clicking in your text anywhere on the screen. Sometime if the sheet is big then you cannot see a place where you want to move. In such situations, you would have to use the scroll bars, we can scroll your sheet by rolling your mouse wheel, which is equivalent to clicking the up-arrow or down-arrow buttons in the scroll bar.

Moving with Scroll Bars

As shown in the above screen capture, there are two scroll bars: one for moving vertically within the sheet, and one for moving horizontally. Using the vertical scroll bar, you may:

Move upward by one line by clicking the upward-pointing scroll arrow.

Move downward by one line by clicking the downward-pointing scroll arrow.

Move one next page, using next page button.

Move one previous page, using previous page button.

Use *Browse Object* button to move through the sheet, going from one chosen object to the next.

Moving with Keyboard

The following keyboard commands, used for moving around your sheet, also move the insertion point:

Keystroke	Where the Insertion Point Moves
→	Forward one box
←	Back one box
↑	Up one box
↓	Down one box
PageUp	To the previous screen
PageDown	To the next screen
Home	To the beginning of the current screen
End	To the end of the current screen

You can move box by box or sheet by sheet. Now click in any box containing data in the sheet. You would have to hold down the Ctrl key while pressing an arrow key, which moves the insertion point as described here:

Built In Functions

MS Excel has many built in functions, which we can use in our formula. To see all the functions by category, choose *Formulas Tab » Insert Function*. Then Insert function Dialog appears from which we can choose the function.

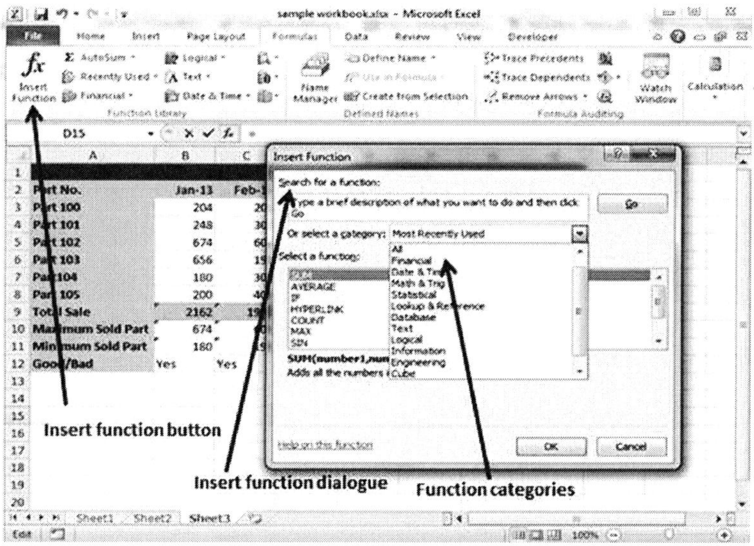

Functions by Categories

Let us see some of the built in functions in MS Excel.

Text Functions

- *Lower:* Converts all characters in a supplied text string to lowercase
- *Upper:* Converts all characters in a supplied text string to uppercase

- *Trim:* Removes duplicate spaces, and spaces at the start and end of a text string.
- *Concatenate:* Joins together two or more text strings.
- *Left:* Returns a specified number of characters from the start of a supplied text string.
- *Mid:* Returns a specified number of characters from the middle of a supplied text string.
- *Right:* Returns a specified number of characters from the end of a supplied text string.
- *Len:* Returns the length of a supplied text string.
- *Find:* Returns the position of a supplied character or text string from within a supplied text string (case-sensitive).

Date & Time

- *Date:* Returns a date, from a user-supplied year, month and day.
- *Time:* Returns a time, from a user-supplied hour, minute and second.
- *Date Value:* Converts a text string showing a date, to an integer that represents the date in Excel's date-time code.
- *Time Value:* Converts a text string showing a time, to a decimal that represents the time in Excel.
- *Now:* Returns the current date & time.
- *Today:* Returns today's date.

Statistical

- *Max:* Returns the largest value from a list of supplied numbers.
- *Min:* Returns the smallest value from a list of supplied numbers.
- *Average:* Returns the Average of a list of supplied numbers.
- *Count:* Returns the number of numerical values in a supplied set of cells or values.
- *Count if:* Returns the number of cells (of a supplied range), that satisfies a given criteria.
- *Sum:* Returns the sum of a supplied list of numbers.

Logical

- *And:* Tests a number of user-defined conditions and returns TRUE if ALL of the conditions evaluate to TRUE, or FALSE otherwise.
- *Or:* Tests a number of user-defined conditions and returns TRUE if ANY of the conditions evaluate to TRUE, or FALSE otherwise.
- *Not:* Returns a logical value that is the opposite of a user supplied logical value or expression i.e. returns FALSE if the supplied argument is TRUE and returns TRUE if the supplied argument is FALSE).

Math & Trig

- *ABS:* Returns the absolute value (i.e. the modulus) of a supplied number.
- *Sign:* Returns the sign (+1, -1 or 0) of a supplied number.
- *Sqrt:* Returns the positive square root of a given number.
- *Mod:* Returns the remainder from a division between two supplied numbers.

Data Filters in MS Excel

Filtering data in MS Excel refers to displaying only the rows that meet certain conditions. (The other rows get hidden.)

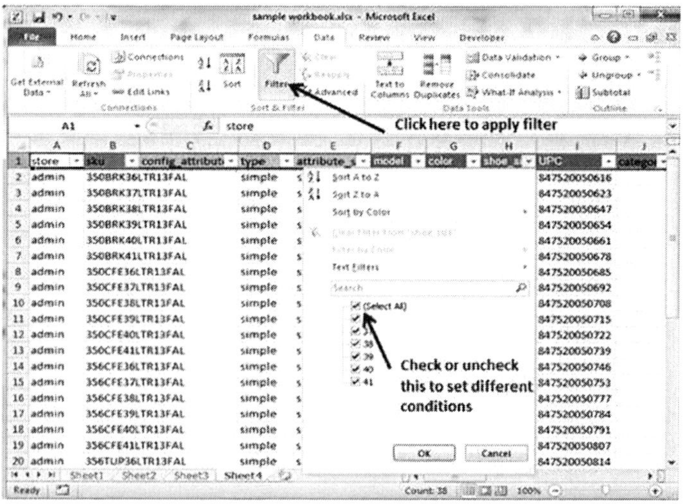

Using the store data, if you are interested in seeing data where Shoe Size is 36, then you can set filter to do this. Follow the below mentioned steps to do this.

- Place a cursor on the Header Row.
- Choose Data Tab » Filter to set filter.

Click the drop—down arrow in the Area Row Header and remove the check mark from Select All, which unselects everything.

Then select the check mark for Size 36, which will filter the data and displays data of Shoe Size 36.

Some of the row numbers are missing; these rows contain the filtered (hidden) data.

There is drop—down arrow in the Area column now shows a different graphic—an icon that indicates the column is filtered.

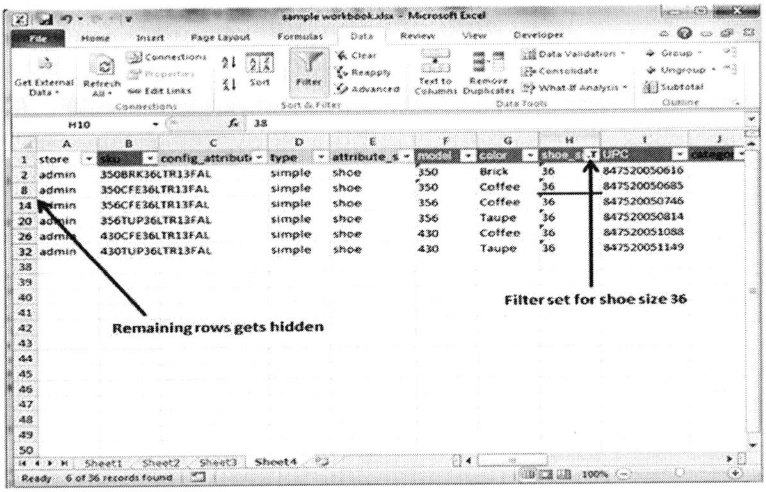

Using Multiple Filters

You can filter the records by multiple conditions i.e. by multiple column values. Suppose after size 36 is filtered, you need to have the filter where color is equal to Coffee. After setting filter for Shoe Size, choose Color column and then set filter for color.

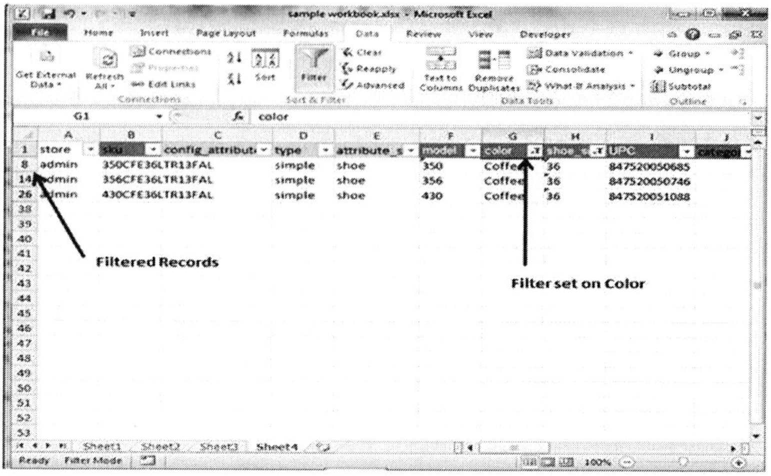

Sorting in MS Excel

Sorting data in MS Excel rearranges the rows based on the contents of a particular column. You may want to sort a table to put names in alphabetical order or, maybe you want to sort data by amount from smallest to largest or largest to smallest.

To sort the data follow the steps mentioned below.

Select the column by which you want to sort data.
Choose Data Tab » sort below dialog appears.

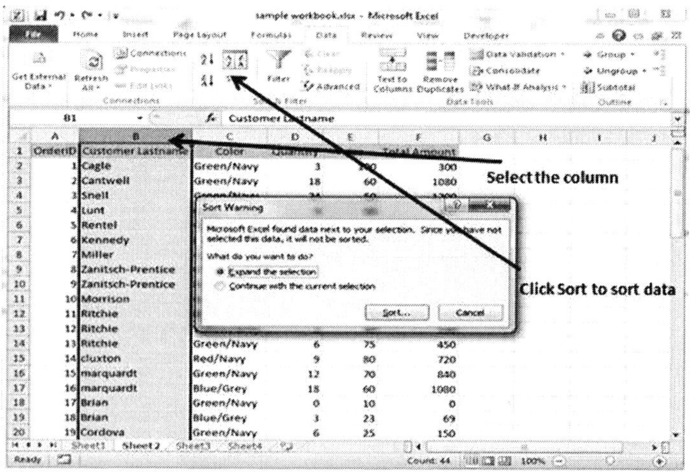

If you want to sort data based on a selected column, choose continue with the selection or if you want sorting based on other columns, choose Expand Selection.

You can Sort based on the below Conditions.

- Values: Alphabetically or numerically.
- Cell Color: Based on Color of Cell.
- Font Color: Based on Font color.
- Cell Icon: Based on Cell Icon.

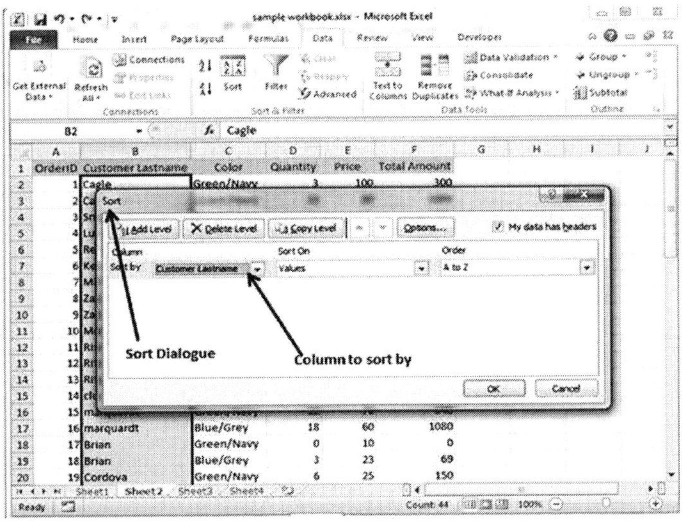

Clicking Ok will sort the data.

Sorting option is also available from the Home Tab. Choose Home Tab » Sort & Filter. You can see the same dialog to sort records

Ranges in MS Excel

A cell is a single element in a worksheet that can hold a value, some text, or a formula. A cell is identified by its address, which consists of its column letter and row number. For example, cell B1 is the cell in the second column and the first row.

A group of cells is called a range. You designate a range address by specifying its upper-left cell address and its lower-right cell address, separated by a colon

Example of Ranges:

C24: A range that consists of a single cell.

A1:B1: Two cells that occupy one row and two columns.

A1:A100: 100 cells in column A.

A1:D4: 16 cells (four rows by four columns).

Selecting Ranges

You can select a range in several ways:

- Press the left mouse button and drag, highlighting the range. Then release the mouse button. If you drag to the end of the screen, the worksheet will scroll.
- Press the Shift key while you use the navigation keys to select a range.
- Press F8 and then move the cell pointer with the navigation keys to highlight the range. Press F8 again to return the navigation keys to normal movement.
- Type the cell or range address into the Name box and press Enter. Excel selects the cell or range that you specified.

Selecting Complete Rows and Columns

When you need to select an entire row or column. You can select entire rows and columns in much the same manner as you select ranges:

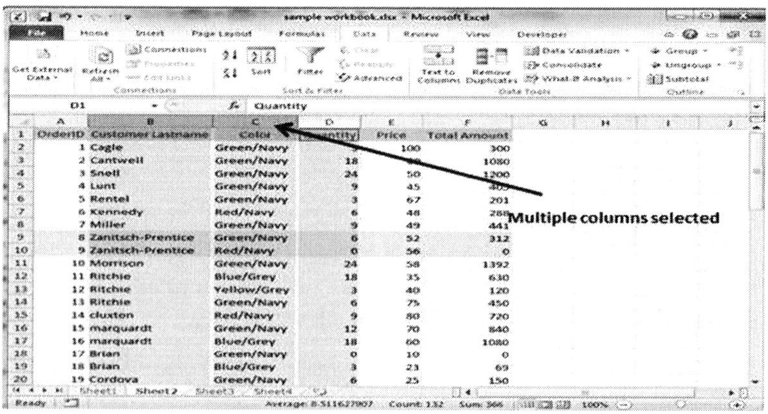

- Click the row or column border to select a single row or column.
- To select multiple adjacent rows or columns, click a row or column border and drag to highlight additional rows or columns.
- To select multiple (nonadjacent) rows or columns, press Ctrl while you click the row or column borders that you want.

Data Validation

MS Excel data validation feature allows you to set up certain rules that dictate what can be entered into a cell. For example, you may want to limit data entry in a particular cell to whole numbers between 0 and 10. If the user makes an invalid entry, you can display a custom message as shown below.

Validation Criteria

To specify the type of data allowable in a cell or range, follow the steps below, which shows all the three tabs of the Data Validation dialog box.

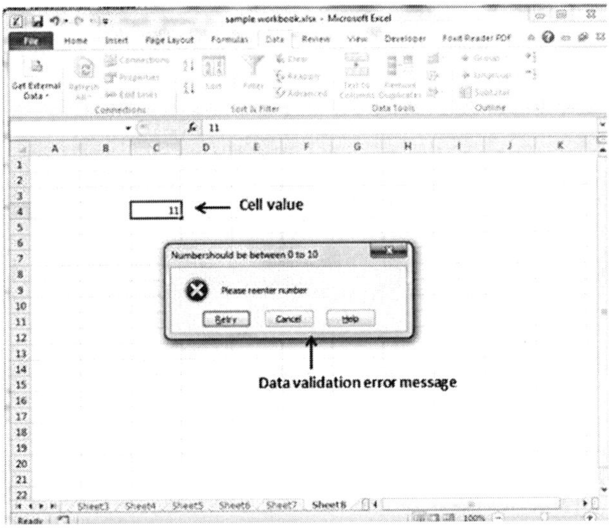

- Select the cell or range.

- Choose Data » Data Tools » Data Validation. Excel displays its Data Validation dialog box having 3 tabs settings, Input Message and Error alert.

Settings Tab

Here you can set the type of validation you need. Choose an option from the Allow drop-down list. The contents of the Data Validation dialog box will change, displaying controls based on your choice.

- **Any Value:** Selecting this option removes any existing data validation.
- **Whole Number:** The user must enter a whole number. For example, you can specify that the entry must be a whole number greater than or equal to 20.
- **Decimal:** The user must enter a number. For example, you can specifyt hat the entry must be greater than or equal to 10 and less than or equal to 15.
- **List:** The user must choose from a list of entries you provide. You will create drop-down list with this validation. You have to give input ranges then those values will appear in the drop-down.
- **Date:** The user must enter a date. You specify a valid date range from choices in the Data drop-down list. For example, you can specify that the entered data must be greater than or equal to January 1, 2018, and less than or equal to December 31, 2018.
- **Time:** The user must enter a time. You specify a valid time range from choices in the Data drop-down list. For example, you can specify that the entered data must be later than 12:00 p.m.
- **Text Length:** The length of the data (number of characters) is limited. You specify a valid length by using the Data drop-down list. For example, you can specify that the length of the entered data be 1 (a single alphanumeric character).
- **Custom:** To use this option, you must supply a logical formula that determines the validity of the user's entry (a logical formula returns either TRUE or FALSE).

Input Message Tab

You can set the input help message with this tab. Fill the title and Input message of the "Input message tab" and the input message will appear when the cell is selected.

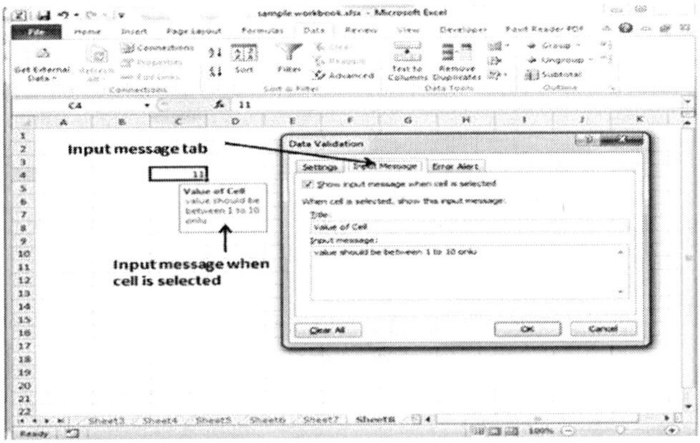

Error Alert Tab

You can specify an error message with this tab. Fill the title and error message. Select the style of the error as stop, warning or Information as per you need.

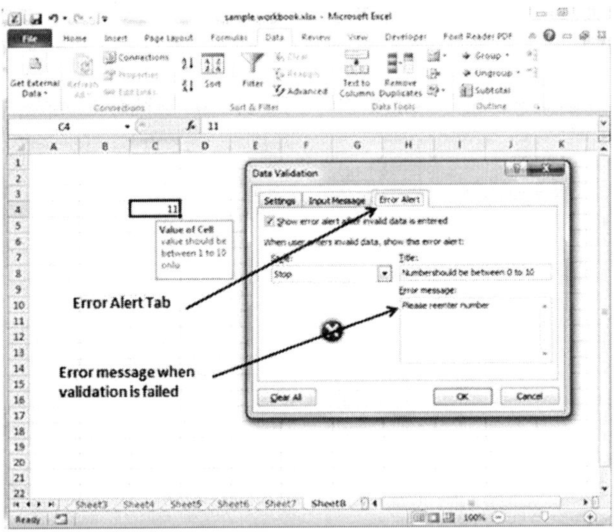

Chapter 4

Mathematical and Statistical Functions in Ms-Excel

Formula Bar

A very important feature in Excel is the formula bar. It is used to calculate values based on what is in cells, perform operations on a cell content, fetch values after an operation based on your search criteria and much more.

Mathematical Formulas in Excel are used to perform various arithmetic operations like sum, average, count, max, min etc. Here is a list of most frequently used mathematical formulas in excel.

By clicking on the equals sign in the formula bar a drop-down panel called the formula bar appeared.

Consider an example, type number 16 in cell A1 and move the cell pointer to cell B2. type or click the equal sign in the formula bar. A drop - down panel will display formula result = and wait for further inputs. Enter sqrt result to 4 at B.

The dialog box divides into parts as:-

a) Name of the function at the top left of the argument entry box.

b) Below of this there is the definition or description of the function.
c) Next, there is an entry explanation.
d) Formula result.

Things to remember: Any statistical or mathematical function can be activate with = (equal to) sign.

Mathematical Functions/Statistical Functions

TODAY () and NOW ()

The syntax is = Today ()
= Now ( )
TODAY ( ) will display the date of the day.

The NOW ( ) functions is the same as TODAY ( ) but in addition it also shows the time.

The Date Function

The syntax is
= DATE (Year, month, day) in (4,2,2) digits.

The date 26th January 2019 will be entered as DATE (2019, 01, 26) will be shown in active cell as 01/26/2019 in American format (which is the default setting). In order to change the format, right click on the date cell and do the following steps:
Format→cells→Date to select the desired format or
Format→Cells→Custom and insert the desired format.

The Sum Function (Σ) or Auto Sum

The syntax is
= SUM (Cell range)
where cell range is the range of cells containing the numbers whose sum is to be calculated.

Exponential Function

The syntax is = EXP (number)

where number is the number whose exponential is need to be calculate. EXP (number) is the value of the natural constant &raised to the power number.

For number = 1, the value is 2.7182818 after pressing the enter means (e^1 = 2.7782818)

For number =2, the value is 7.389056 after pressing the enter means (e^2 = 7.389056)

The Logarithm

The Natural Logarithm Function

The syntax is

= LN (number)

where number is a real positive number whose natural log is required. The natural log is the inverse of the exponential, i.e. LN (2.7182818), is equal to 1 and LN (7.389056) is equal to 2.

Log to the Base 10

The syntax is

= LOG 10 (number)

For number = 15, the value is 1.176091

Log to any Base

The syntax is

= log (number, base)

Number must be real and positive.

=Log (125,5) the value is 3.

=Log (64,2718) equal to 4.159314.

Square root function

The syntax is

= SQRT (number)

SQRT (64) result to 8 after pressing enter.

Factorial Functions

The syntax is

=FACT (number)

Result to the factorial of a real positive natural number.

=FACT (0) results to 1,

=FACT (10) results to 3628800

The Binomial Coefficient

The syntax is

= COMB IN (n,r)

where n and r are the two numbers as defined in the binomial coefficient formula above.

COMBIN (3,0) result to the value 1 and COMBIN (3,1) result to the value 3.

Trigonometric Functions

The syntax for the sine, cosine and tangent function is as

SIN (number)

COS (number)

TAN (number)

Inverse Trigonometric Functions

The syntax for sine inverse is = SIN^{-1} or ASIN (number)

Matrix Mathematics

Determinant of a Matrix

The syntax is

= MDETERM (array)

Where array is the range of cells that contains the element of a square matrix.

The Transpose of Matrix

The syntax is

= TRANSPOSE (array)

Where array is the cell range or array of numbers which is to be transposed. The area for the required matrix should be selected in advance then type the syntax, Press Ctrl + Shift + Enter simultaneously.

For example, consider a matrix of order 4x3 in the excel data as below sheet.

A	=	2	4	6
		5	7	8
		1	5	4
		9	6	2

Then select the area of cells of order 3x4, type syntax - Transpose (array), select the array and Press

Ctrl + Shift + Enter result to A^T.

A^T	=	2	5	1	9
		4	7	5	6
		6	8	4	2

It can also be done through Paste special command. Follow the following steps

i) Copy the array of Matrix
ii) Select the area
iii) Paste Special→Select Transpose→ok. [Right click on the cell]

Matrix Multiplications

The syntax is

— MMULT (array 1, array2)

Where array 1 and array 2 are the two matrices that are to be multiplied. It must be noted that the number of columns of array 1 is equal to the numbers of rows of array 2. The resultant matrix number of rows and number of columns of array 1 and array 2 respectively.

Steps

1. Select two matrices.
2. Select the area for resultant matrix.
3. Type = MMULT (array of 1st matrix, array of 2nd matrix)
4. Press Ctrl + Shift + Enter.

Matrix A =

2	4	6
5	7	8
1	5	4
9	6	2

Matrix B =

5	6	2	1
7	5	3	2
3	5	4	1

Resultant matrix (AxB) =

56	62	40
98	105	63
52	51	33
93	94	44

Matrix Inverse

The syntax is

= MINVERSE (array)

Where array is the cell range specifying the original matrix. The matrix must be square means number of rows and number of columns of matrix must be same.

1. Consider a square matrix.
2. Select the area for resultant matrix same as the original matrix.
3. Type = MINVERSE (array).
4. Select array i.e. matrix whose inverse is to find.
5. Press Ctrl + Shift + Enter.

Matix A=

2	6	8
10	3	5
0	12	6

Inverse of Matrix A^{-1}=

-0.0814	0.116279	0.011628
-0.11628	0.023256	0.135659
0.232558	-0.04651	-0.10465

Some Statistical Functions

Average

The syntax is
= AVERAGE (cell range)
where cell range is the range of cells of the numbers whose average is need to be calculated.

Geometric Mean

The syntax is
= GEOMEAN (cell range)
where cell range are cells that contain the number whose geometric mean is to be calculated.

Harmonic Mean

Its syntax is
= HARMEAN (number 1, number 2, number 3)
Where number 1, number 2 and number 3 are for which Harmonic mean is to be calculated.

Standard Deviation

The syntax of the standard deviation is = STDEV (Cell range).

The Square of the Deviations from the Mean

The syntax is DEVSQ (Cell range).

Percentage

In order to calculate the percentage of the amount of money spent per month, we sum up the expenditure of 12 months and divided by total number of months.

A	B	C	D
S. No	Month	Spending	Percentage
1.	January	7025	=(C2/C$14)*100
2.	February	6125	
3.	March	7100	
4.	April	7150	

A	B	C	D
5.	May	7180	
6.	June	9000	
7.	July	9050	
8.	August	7500	
9.	September	7750	
10.	October	9500	
11.	November	7600	
12.	December	9000	
Total		**93980**	

Percentage = (C2/C$14)*100

Type the above formulae in D1 cell and drag up to D13 will result to the percentage.

Random Number

Microsoft excels having two following useful functions while creating random numbers as:

RAND

For creating the decimal numbers between 0 to 1, Steps:

1. Select the cell A1.
2. Type RAND () and press Enter. The RAND function takes no arguments.
3. Now for creating list of random numbers, select cell A1 and click on the lower right corner of cell A1 and drag it down.

A1
0.116216
0.156046
0.241796
0.556355
0.748585
0.790927
0.857495

Rand Between

For creating whole numbers between two boundaries Steps:

1. Select the cell C1
2. Type Rand BETWEEN (40, 70) and press Enter
3. For creating random decimal numbers between 40 and 70, modify the RAND function to =40+30*RAND().
4. Drag the lower right comer for various decimal numbers.

=RandBetween(40,70)	= 40+30*RAND()
51	53.16018
64	46.22142
59	58.01956
66	59.22261
40	48.67188
49	47.05443
53	57.26114
54	47.82712

Rank

Steps:

1. Consider the data in Column A.
2. Type = Rank (Input data) on B1
3. Drag the Rank function down the absolute reference stay the same, while the relative reference A1 changes to A2, A3, and A4 etc.

=Rank(60,A1:A8)

A1	B2
60	5
70	2
50	5
30	5
65	2
55	3
65	2
75	1

Common Problems with Formula and Values (Debugging errors)

Troubleshooting an Excel worksheet's formulas and functions can be a big job. Errors just come with the package. Excel offers some valuable auditing tools, found on the Formulas tab in the Formula Auditing group, but you won't always need that much power. Sometimes, just a bit of special knowledge can help you resolve an error.

1. Excel Error—#NAME?

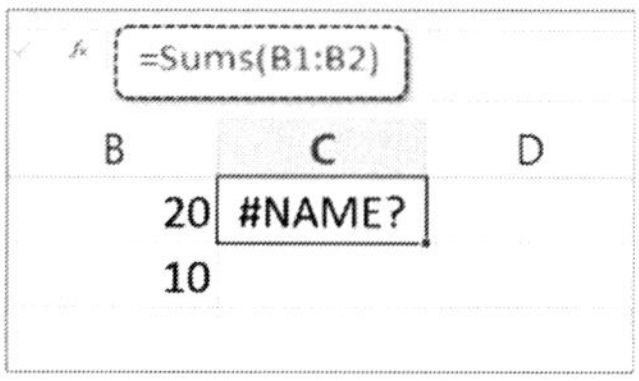

You may have noticed #NAME? Error several times and this can appear for various reasons. The most common being misspelt formula in the above example the formula SUM is misspelt as SUMS]. Here are few more common reasons which one could look out and avoid this error:

- ✶ A formula that doesn't exist.
- ✶ Misspelt references and ranges.
- ✶ Text entered without enclosing double quotation marks.
- ✶ Range defined without colon (:)

2. Excel Error—#REF!

This type of error occurs basically when one makes an invalid cell reference. Let's take an example. Say we have 3 columns which have few values.

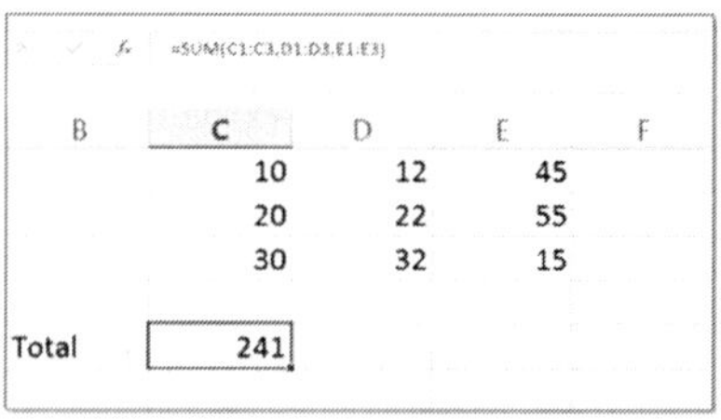

Now when I delete column E, then the range "E1:E3" referred in the formula is no longer valid and will produce the #REF! Error.

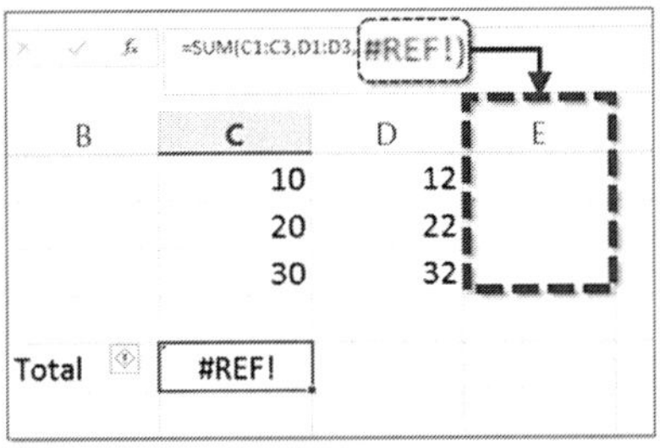

Few more common reasons which one could look out and avoid this error: Copy/paste cells above the cells referred by formula, thus making an invalid cell reference. Using OLE (Object Linking and Embedding) link to a program that's no longer valid or not running.

3. Excel Error – #DIV/0!

A simple mathematical theory says any number when divided by zero produces infinity. EXCEL does this by producing #DIV/0! error. Thus, in EXCEL whenever the formula attempts to divide by a zero this error would appear.

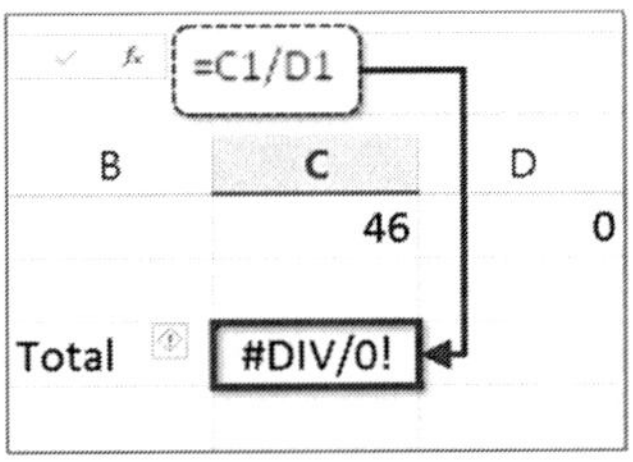

In the above example, we are attempting to divide C1 (46) by D1 (0) and hence the excel error.

The other common reason which one could look out to avoid this kind of an error: There could be a chance that you have left divisor cell empty then the same error would appear. For example, in the below scenario, the divisor (D1) was empty and hence the error.

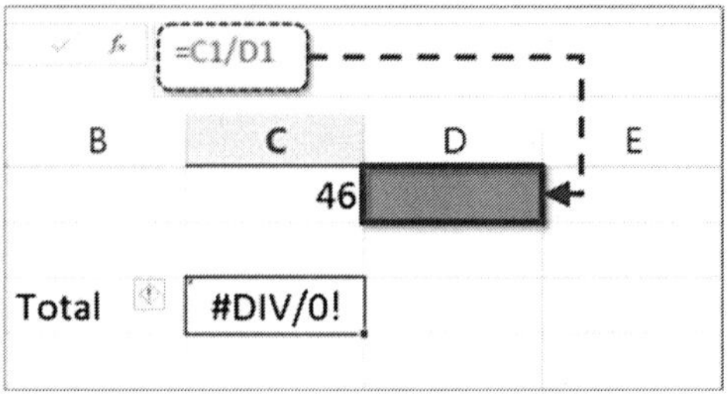

4. Excel Error—#N/A

There are several reasons for this error to occur. But the most generic one is passing an unavailable value to the formula. As the below example shows, that an inappropriate value 'Z' is being passed to VLOOKUP function and hence the error, whereas for the same case if you pass an appropriate value i.e. 'A' or 'B' or 'C' to VLOOKUP function, you get respective values instead of #N/A error.

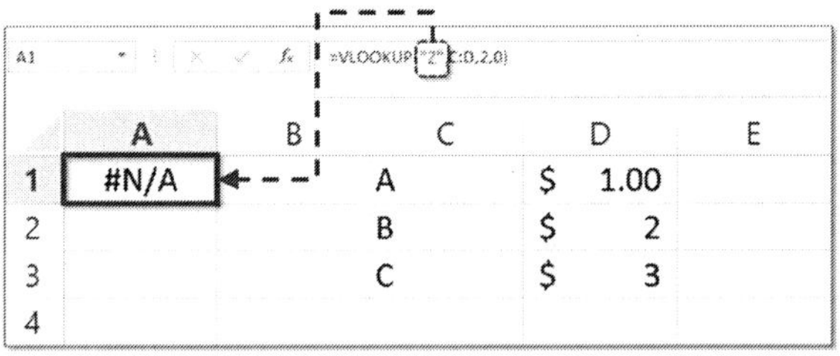

The other reasons which one could look out to avoid this kind of an error: Missing data. Inappropriate lookup value being passed to VLOOKUP, HLOOKUP or MATCH function. Use of N/A or NA as a part of data.

5. Excel Error—#NULL!

This type of error occurs when you try to provide a range that does not intersect each other. In the below example, we have specified two different ranges to the formula. But since these two ranges are independent of each other and have no intersection, it results in #NULL! Error.

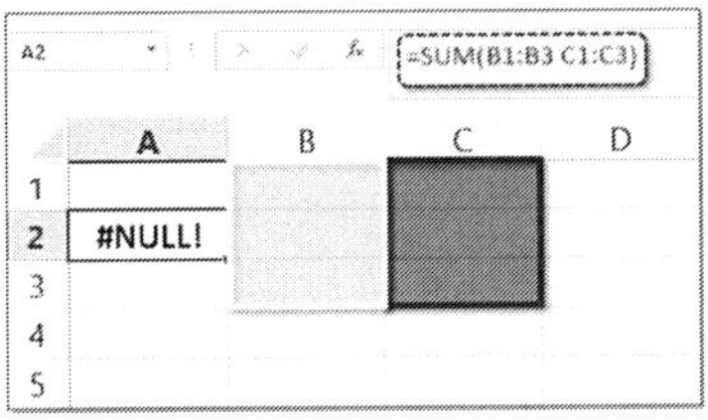

Given the same scenario, if the range specified were SUM (B1: B3 A1: C1), it would have resulted in a value. This is due to a fact that an intersection is happening between two ranges at the cell B1. Given below is an example of a valid range with an intersection point. The same has been missing in the above example and hence the NULL error.

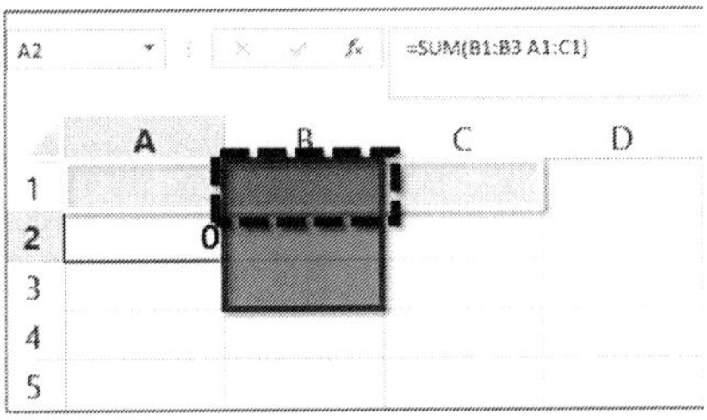

The other common reason which one could look out to avoid this kind of an error: • When the cell ranges are defined improperly like missing colons(:) or space instead of mathematical operators.

6. Excel Error—#NUM!

The general trend for #NUM! Error to occur is when an EXCEL comes across a large value.

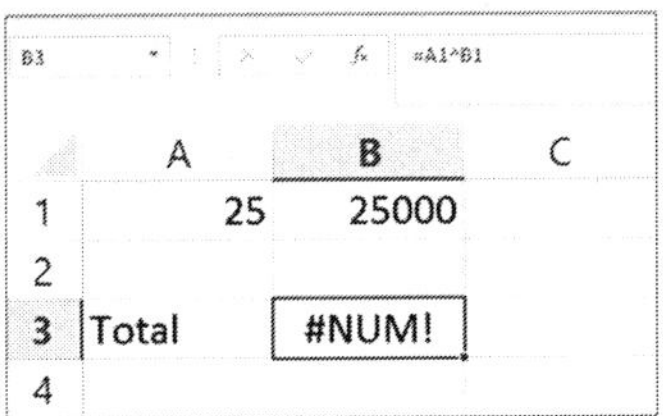

In the above example, the calculation is too large for EXCEL to handle and hence it returns #NUM! error. The other common reason which one could look out to avoid this kind of an error: Passing wrong data/data type to a function. Like SQRT (4) function returns 2 but using the same function for negative values doesn't make much sense and EXCEL, in this case, will return #NUM! error.

7. Excel Error—#VALUE!

This error occurs when the variables specified to a function are of wrong types.

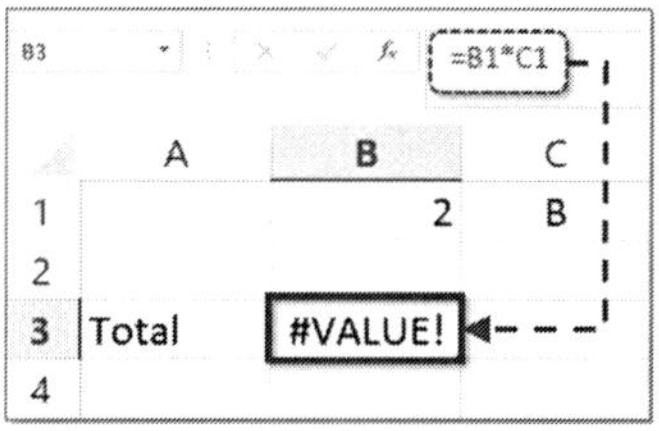

In the above example, two values are being multiplied while one being numeric ('2' in cell B1), the other being a char ('B' in cell C1). This results in a mismatch of data type and hence the #VALUE! error. The other common reason which one could look out to avoid this kind of an error: Use of mathematical formula like SUM, MUL etc... which takes input as a number but chars or strings are being passed to it.

8. Excel Error—######

This error occurs when your EXCEL column is not wide enough to accommodate a large value. For example, if a long number like 123123456456789789 is set to occupy a small cell then it would show up as #### error. Widening the cell in can eradicate the error in above case but there are few more scenarios where this error can appear: Result doesn't fit in the cell. If a negative number has been formatted to date or time then it will also produce this

error. The reason being date and time are always supposed to be positive.

9. Excel Error—Circular Reference

This error is rarest of all the errors to occur but can get you tangled in the web. This basically occurs when you define a result on a cell, which is also a part of one of your formula. For example, in perfect conditions, I would plan to add values from range A2 to A6 with its total at cell A7. This would work just like any other normal formula function. But what if I specify the result at cell A6 instead of A7. A6 being part of SUM range itself. Then I get into *circular references* and this error might lead to wrong results.

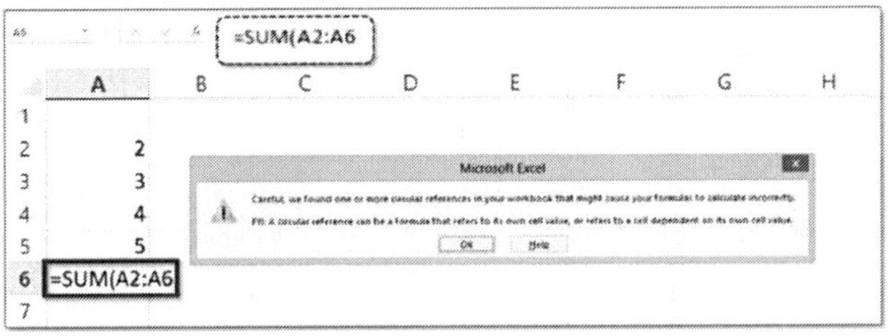

The best way to overcome this to assign the results to a different cell and try to keep values and results as different as possible.

The Green Triangle

If you see a green triangle appearing on the top-left corner of the resultant cell, it's an indication that something has gone wrong with the formula. If you are not sure of the error, simply click the error cell. An !mark with a drop-down arrow will appear.

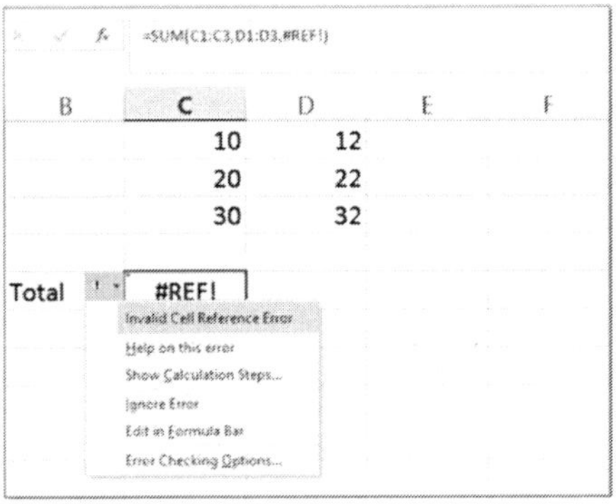

This will point out the nature of the error and will also give you further options for evaluation. If you are still not sure or having a difficult time locating an error, you can use Trace Error or Circular

Reference option [*navigate to FORMULAS tab→Error Checking dropdown→Trace Error | Circular Reference option*].

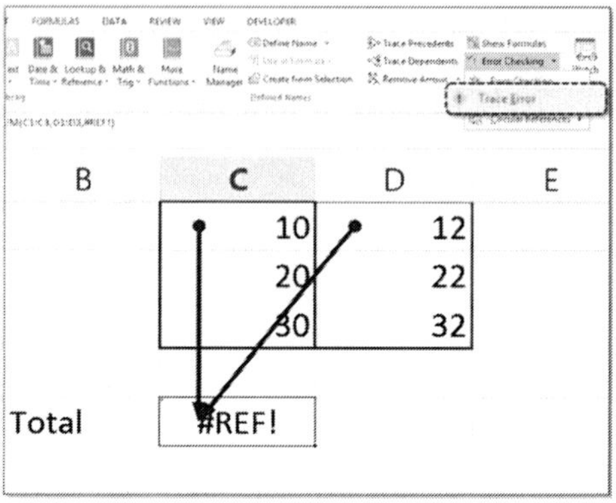

This will point out the error and the cell and you can then determine as to what went wrong.

Chapter 5

Data Analysis Using MS-Excel

Microsoft Excel is one of the tools for data analysis and the built-in pivot tables are arguably the most popular analytic tools.

In this chapter, you will learn how to perform data analysis using Excel's most popular features. You will learn how to create pivot tables from a range with rows and columns in Excel. You will see the power of Excel pivots in action and their ability to summarize data in flexible ways, enabling quick exploration of data and producing valuable insights from the accumulated data.

Pivots are used by millions of users who share the goal of reporting the performance of organizations. In addition, Excel formulas can be used to aggregate data to create meaningful reports. To complement, pivot charts and slicers can be used together to visualize data and create easy to use dashboards.

Summary Statistics

The following data are the marks in statistics of 36 students:

72, 74, 85, 96, 87, 67, 53, 74, 89, 65, 88, 65, 45, 70, 25, 80, 75, 85, 47, 63, 78, 44, 42, 51, 59, 86, 76, 48, 30, 38, 67, 78, 74, 68, 58, 59.

Calculate the descriptive statistics for the study of the data.

Solution: The descriptive statistics of the data using MS excel can be obtained / analyzed through following steps:

Step 1: Open Excel sheet and feed the data.

Step 2: Go to data menu and select Data Analysis. Sometimes this menu is not available in the data, it can be added through add in→check in, analysis tool pack go.

Step 3: Select analysis tool from Data Analysis dialog box.

Step 4: Give input range in descriptive statistics dialog box.

Step 5: Give output range in Output options for getting output in specific range of cells

Step 6: Check in Summary statistics and level in first column boxes

Step 7: Click on OK command button and output will be obtained

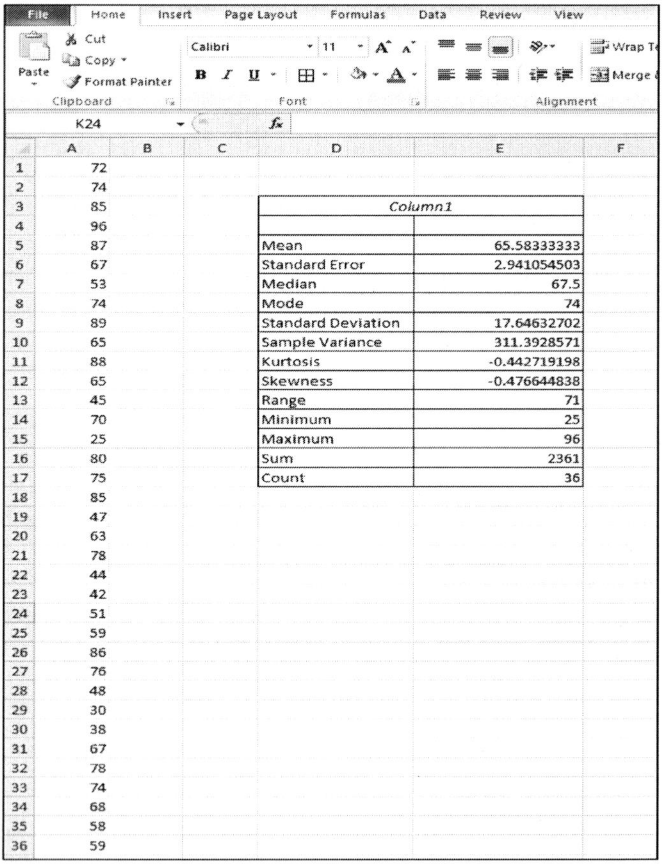

Correlation

From a paddy field, 12 plants were selected at random. The length of panicles in cm (x) and the number of grains per panicle (y) of the selected plants were recorded. The results are given in the following table. Calculate correlation coefficient and its testing.

y	112	131	147	90	110	106	127	145	85	95	142	111
x	22.9	23.9	24.8	21.2	22.2	22.7	23.0	24.0	20.6	21.0	24.0	23.1

Step 1: Open Excel sheet and feed the data as given.

Step 2: Go to data menu and select Data Analysis.

Step 3: Select Analysis tool from Data Analysis dialog box.

Step 4: Give input range in Correlation dialog box.

Step 5: Give output range in Output options for getting output in specific range of cells.

Step 6: Click on OK command button for output.

Thus the correlation between length of panicles in cm and the number of grains per panicle is 0.951285.

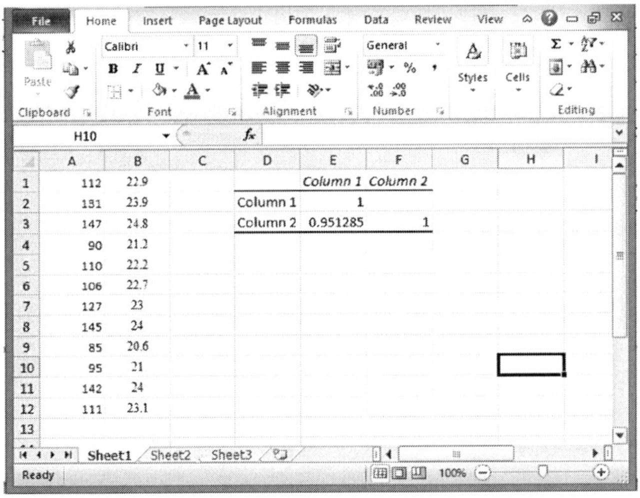

Regression

The following data for the amount of water supplied in inches and the yield of alfalfa in tones per acre.

Water (X)	12	18	24	30	36	42	48
Yield (Y)	5.3	5.7	6.7	7.2	8.2	8.7	8.4

Find the regression of yield on water. Assuming that, the relation between the two is linear. Calculate the expected yield when the amount of water supplied is 20 inches.

Solution: The regression analysis output can be obtained through following steps.

Step 1: Open Excel sheet and feed the data as given.

Step 2: Go to data menu and select Data Analysis.

Step 3: Select Analysis tools form Data Analysis dialog box.

Step 4: Give input range in regression dialog box.

Step 5: Give output range in Output options for getting output in specific range of cells.

Step 6: Click the Ok command button for output.

Conclusions: From the output it is found that the regression model was adequate as compared to the mean model. Further it is observed that R^2 was 0.93 which indicate that there is 93% variation in yield of alfalfa due to change in amount of water supplied. The estimated regression equation is

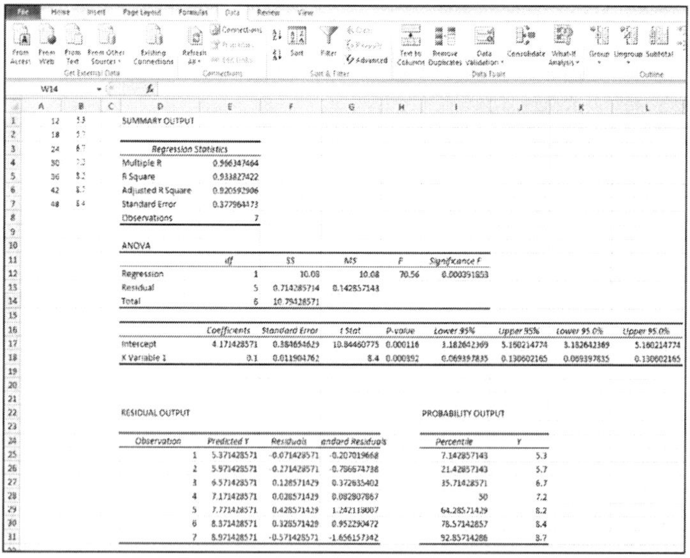

SUMMARY OUTPUT

Regression Statistics	
Multiple R	0.966347464
R Square	0.933827422
Adjusted R Square	0.920592906
Standard Error	0.377964473
Observations	7

ANOVA

	df	SS	MS	F	Significance F
Regression	1	10.08	10.08	70.56	0.000391853
Residual	5	0.714285714	0.142857143		
Total	6	10.79428571			

	Coefficients	Standard Error	t Stat	P-value	Lower 95%	Upper 95%	Lower 95.0%	Upper 95.0%
Intercept	4.171428571	0.384654629	10.84460775	0.000116	3.182642369	5.160214774	3.182642369	5.160214774
X Variable 1	0.1	0.011904762	8.4	0.000392	0.069397835	0.130602165	0.069397835	0.130602165

RESIDUAL OUTPUT

Observation	Predicted Y	Residuals	andard Residuals
1	5.371428571	-0.071428571	-0.207019668
2	5.971428571	-0.271428571	-0.786674738
3	6.571428571	0.128571429	0.372635402
4	7.171428571	0.028571429	0.082807867
5	7.771428571	0.428571429	1.242119007
6	8.371428571	0.328571429	0.952290472
7	8.971428571	-0.571428571	-1.656157342

PROBABILITY OUTPUT

Percentile	Y
7.142857143	5.3
21.42857143	5.7
35.71428571	6.7
50	7.2
64.28571429	8.2
78.57142857	8.4
92.85714286	8.7

*Y^ = 4.17** +0.1 **X. Further if X = 20inches then Y^ = 4.17+0.1(20) = 6.17 tones/acre.*

t-test and F-test

Two varieties of tomato plants (X and Y) yields are shown in the following table. Does the mean number of tomatoes of the variety 'X' significantly differ from that of variety 'Y'?

Tuber yield, kg/plant

Variety –X	2.0	2.5	1.9	2.4	2.8	2.3	1.8	2.0	2.1	2.4	2.7
Variety –Y	2.6	2.7	2.5	3.0	3.1	2.3	2.5	3.2	2.5	2.8	2.1

Solution

It can be done through the t-test. In analysis tool pack there are two options (i) t-test with equal variances (ii) t-test with unequal variances. Therefore we have to examine which t-test is to be used. This can be tested through the F- test (Levene's test) with the following hypothesis

$$H_0: \sigma_1^2=\sigma_0^2 \text{ vs } H_1: \sigma_0^2\neq\sigma_1^2$$

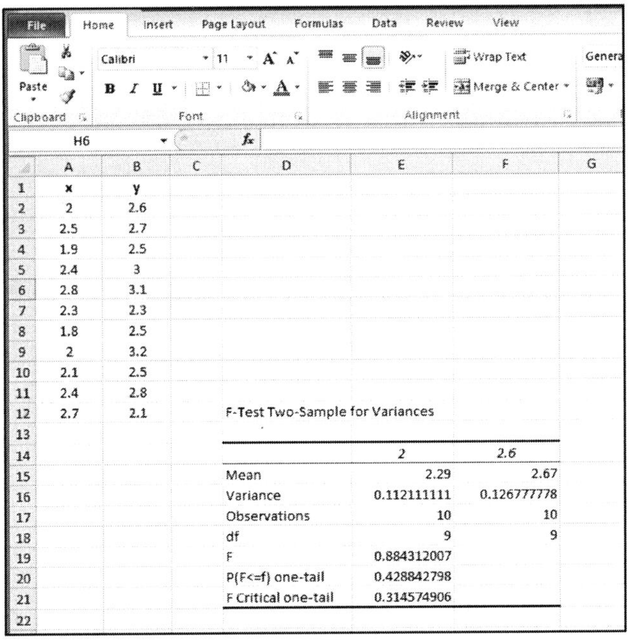

	A	B
1	x	y
2	2	2.6
3	2.5	2.7
4	1.9	2.5
5	2.4	3
6	2.8	3.1
7	2.3	2.3
8	1.8	2.5
9	2	3.2
10	2.1	2.5
11	2.4	2.8
12	2.7	2.1

F-Test Two-Sample for Variances

	2	2.6
Mean	2.29	2.67
Variance	0.112111111	0.126777778
Observations	10	10
df	9	9
F	0.884312007	
P(F<=f) one-tail	0.428842798	
F Critical one-tail	0.314574906	

Case I: F-test for testing the equality of populations' variances

Step 1: Open Excel sheet and feed the data as per data given.

Step 2: Go to data menu and select data Analysis.

Step 3: Select F-test Analysis tool from Data Analysis dialog box.

Step 4: Give input range in F-test: two samples for variance dialog box.

Step 5: Give output range in output options for getting output in specific range of cells

Step 6: Click on OK command button

it is observed from the output that the p-value of the F-test is greater than 0.05. Thus the test is non- significant means accept the null hypothesis. Therefore, we will apply the t-test with equal variances otherwise t-test with unequal variances. Thus the two have the same yield at population level.

Now, Case II: t- test with equal variances for testing the equality of yield of the two varieties.

Step 1: Open Excel sheet and feed the data as given

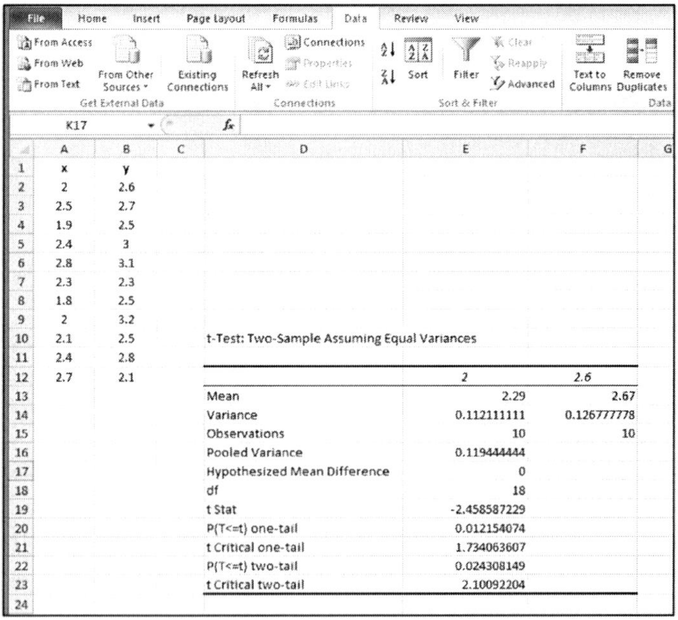

Step 2: Go to data menu and select Data Analysis.

Step 3: Select t-test: two samples assuming equal variances analysis tools from Data Analysis dialog box.

Step 4: Give input range in t-test: two samples assuming equal variances dialog box.

Step 5: Give output range in Output options for getting output n specific range of cells.

Step 6: Click on OK button.

Conclusions: From the output it is observed that the p-value of the t- test is less than 0.05 so the test is significant means reject the null hypothesis. Thus, the two varieties have the different yield.

Paired t-test

The milk yield of ten cows before and after the feed were recorded as

Before	6	8	10	12	11	9	7	10	9	13
After	10	10	11	13	14	10	9	13	12	15

Test whether there is any significant difference between the milk yield before and after the feed

Solution: Here the observations are from the homogenous group hence paired t-test is to be used and the hypothesis is as follow:

$$\mathbf{H_0: \sigma_1^2=\sigma_0^2 \text{ vs } H_1: \sigma_0^2 \neq \sigma_1^2}$$

Step 1: Open Excel sheet and feed the data as given.

Step 2: Go to data menu and select Data Analysis.

Step 3: Select t-test: paired two samples for means analysis tool from Data Analysis dialog box.

Step 4: Give input in t-test: paired two samples for means analysis dialog box.

Step 5: Give output range in Output options for getting output in specific range of cells

Step 6: Click on OK command button.

Conclusions: It can be observed from the output that the t_{cal}>t(9, .05) therefore, null hypothesis is rejected and we concluded that the milk yield differ significantly before and after the feed.

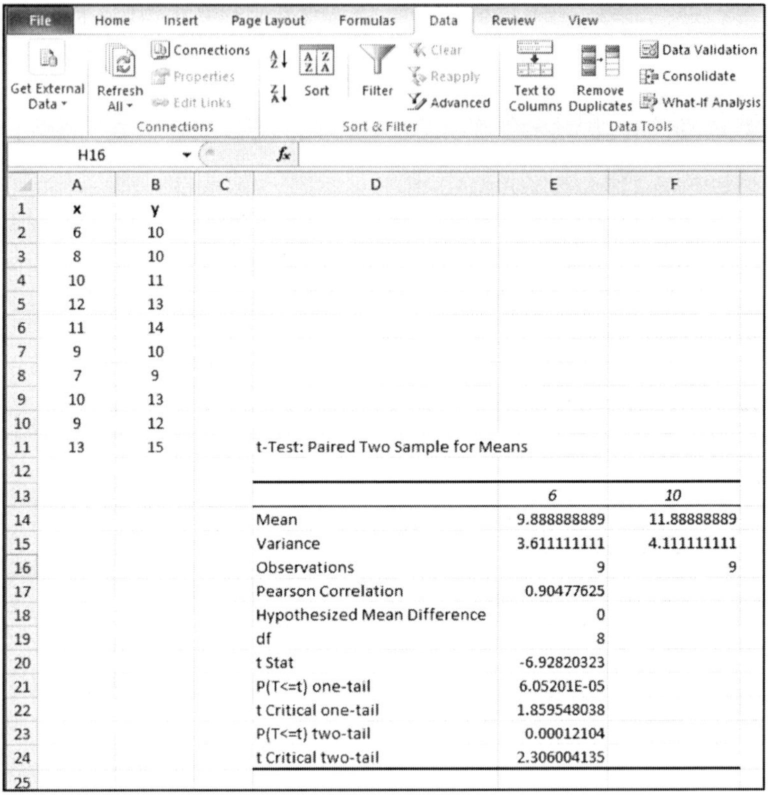

	A	B	C	D	E	F
1	x	y				
2	6	10				
3	8	10				
4	10	11				
5	12	13				
6	11	14				
7	9	10				
8	7	9				
9	10	13				
10	9	12				
11	13	15		t-Test: Paired Two Sample for Means		
12						
13					6	10
14				Mean	9.888888889	11.88888889
15				Variance	3.611111111	4.111111111
16				Observations	9	9
17				Pearson Correlation	0.90477625	
18				Hypothesized Mean Difference	0	
19				df	8	
20				t Stat	-6.92820323	
21				P(T<=t) one-tail	6.05201E-05	
22				t Critical one-tail	1.859548038	
23				P(T<=t) two-tail	0.00012104	
24				t Critical two-tail	2.306004135	
25						

One way ANOVA

A set of data involving four "tropical feed stuffs A, B, C, D" tried on 20 chicks is given below. All the twenty chicks are treated alike in all respects except the feeding treatments and each feeding treatment is given to 5 chicks. Analyse the data

Feed	Gain in Weight					Total Ti
A	55	49	42	21	52	219
B	61	112	30	89	63	355
C	42	97	81	95	92	407

Feed	Gain in Weight					Total Ti
D	169	137	169	85	154	714
	Grand Total					G = 1695

Perform the analysis of variance.

Solution: This is a fixed effect model can be written as:	Yij =μ + αi + eij
The null hypothesis will be	H_0: $\mu_1 = \mu_2$ vs H_1: $\mu_1 \neq \mu_2$

H1: At least one feed stuff differs from other.

Step 1: Open Excel sheet and feed the data as given.

Step 2: Go to data menu and select Data Analysis.

Step 3: Select Anova single factor analysis tool from Data Analysis dialog box.

Step 4: Give input range in Anova single factor analysis dialog box.

Step 5: Give output range in Output options for getting output in specific range of cells.

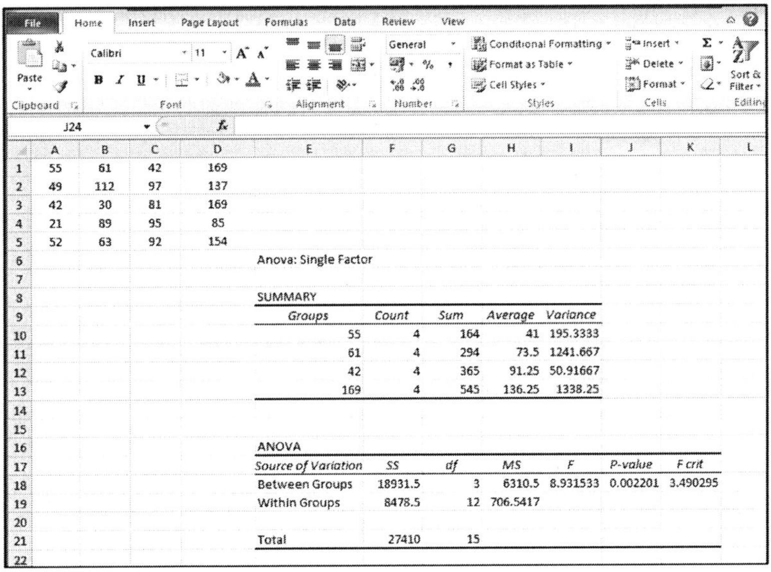

A	B	C	D
55	61	42	169
49	112	97	137
42	30	81	169
21	89	95	85
52	63	92	154

Anova: Single Factor

SUMMARY

Groups	Count	Sum	Average	Variance
55	4	164	41	195.3333
61	4	294	73.5	1241.667
42	4	365	91.25	50.91667
169	4	545	136.25	1338.25

ANOVA

Source of Variation	SS	df	MS	F	P-value	F crit
Between Groups	18931.5	3	6310.5	8.931533	0.002201	3.490295
Within Groups	8478.5	12	706.5417			
Total	27410	15				

Conclusions: From the output it can be observed that F-calculated is greater than F-tabulated and further p-value is less than the level of significance (0.0022) therefore the null hypothesis is rejected which means that the feed stuff differ significantly.

Note: Completely Randomized design (CRD) is a special case of one-way ANOVA. CRD for equal and unequal replications can be done through the same way. The model is Yij =μ + Ti + eij

Another Example of One Way ANOVA

An experiment was conducted in CRD in which Feed A was given to 5 cows, Feed B to 5 cows, Feed C to 5 cows and Feed D to 5 cows. Analyze the data and state your conclusions.

Feed A	Feed B	Feed C	Feed D
24	49	54	64
36	43	50	56
27	42	49	59
28	40	52	57
30	46	54	55

Perform the analysis of variance.

Solution: This is a fixed effect model can be written as:

$Y_{ij} = \mu + \alpha_i + e_{ij}$

$H_0: \mu_1 = \mu_2$ vs $H_1: \mu_1 \neq \mu_2$

The null hypothesis will be

H_1: At least one feed differs from other.

Step 1: Open Excel sheet and feed the data as given.

Step 2: Go to data menu and select Data Analysis.

Step 3: Select Anova single factor analysis tool from Data Analysis dialog box.

Step 4: Give input range in Anova single factor analysis dialog box.

Step 5: Give output range in Output options for getting output in specific range of cells.

Conclusions: From the output it can be observed that F-calculated is greater than F-tabulated and further p-value is less than the level of significance(0.0001) therefore the null hypothesis is rejected which means that the feeds differ significantly.

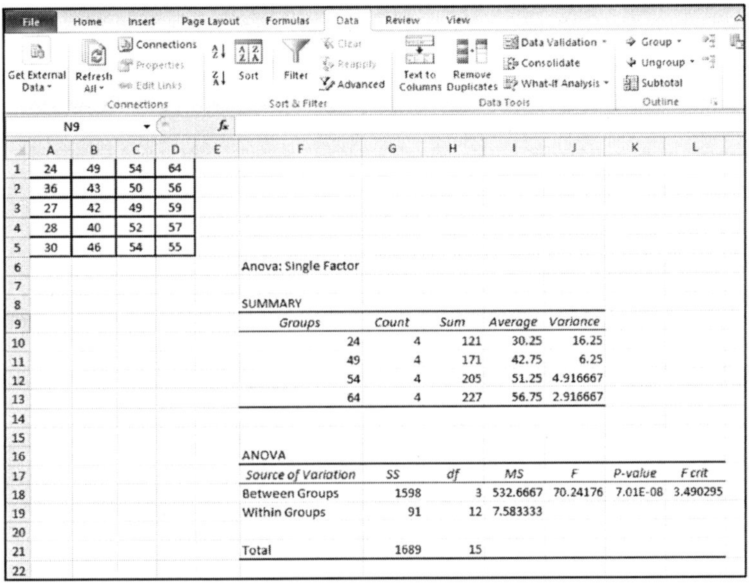

A	B	C	D
24	49	54	64
36	43	50	56
27	42	49	59
28	40	52	57
30	46	54	55

Anova: Single Factor

SUMMARY

Groups	*Count*	*Sum*	*Average*	*Variance*
24	4	121	30.25	16.25
49	4	171	42.75	6.25
54	4	205	51.25	4.916667
64	4	227	56.75	2.916667

ANOVA

Source of Variation	*SS*	*df*	*MS*	*F*	*P-value*	*F crit*
Between Groups	1598	3	532.6667	70.24176	7.01E-08	3.490295
Within Groups	91	12	7.583333			
Total	1689	15				

Two way ANOVA

The yields of 6 varieties of a crop in lbs., along with the plan of the experiment, are given below. The number of blocks is 5, plot of size is 1/20 acre and the varieties have been represented by A, B, C, D and E and analyze the data and state your conclusions.

B-I	B 12	E 26	D 10	C 15	A 26	F 62
B-II	E 23	C 16	F 56	A 30	D 20	B 10
B-III	A 28	B 9	E 35	F 64	D 23	C 14
B-IV	F 75	D 20	E 30	C 14	B 7	A 23
B-V	D 17	F 70	A 20	C 12	B 9	E 28

First rearrange the given data

Blocks	Varieties					
	A	B	C	D	E	F
B1	26	12	15	10	26	62
B2	30	10	16	20	23	56
B3	28	9	14	23	35	64
B4	23	7	14	20	30	75
B5	20	9	12	17	28	70

Analyze the Data

Solution: This can be tested $Y_{ij}=\mu + \alpha_i + \beta_j + e_{ij}$ through fixed effect model which can be written as:

The null hypothesis will be $H_0: \mu_1 = \mu_2$ vs $H_1: \mu_1 \neq \mu_2$
H1: At least one treatment significantly differs from other

The following steps will be used

Step 1: Open Excel sheet and feed the data as given.
Step 2: Go to data menu and select Data Analysis.

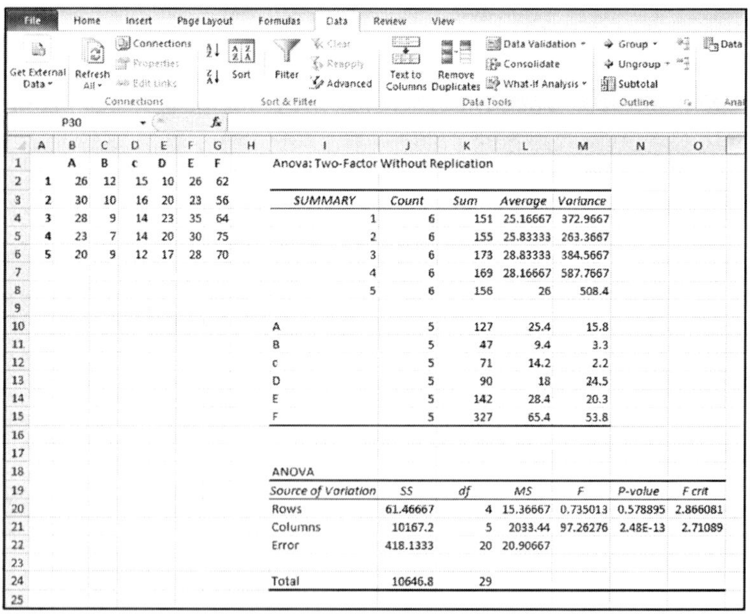

	A	B	C	D	E	F
1	26	12	15	10	26	62
2	30	10	16	20	23	56
3	28	9	14	23	35	64
4	23	7	14	20	30	75
5	20	9	12	17	28	70

Anova: Two-Factor Without Replication

SUMMARY	Count	Sum	Average	Variance
1	6	151	25.16667	372.9667
2	6	155	25.83333	263.3667
3	6	173	28.83333	384.5667
4	6	169	28.16667	587.7667
5	6	156	26	508.4
A	5	127	25.4	15.8
B	5	47	9.4	3.3
C	5	71	14.2	2.2
D	5	90	18	24.5
E	5	142	28.4	20.3
F	5	327	65.4	53.8

ANOVA

Source of Variation	SS	df	MS	F	P-value	F crit
Rows	61.46667	4	15.36667	0.735013	0.578895	2.866081
Columns	10167.2	5	2033.44	97.26276	2.48E-13	2.71089
Error	418.1333	20	20.90667			
Total	10646.8	29				

Step 3: Select anova single two factor without replications tool from Data Analysis dialog box.

Step 4: Give input range in two factor without replications analysis dialog box.

Step 5: Give output range in Output options for getting output in specific range of cells

Conclusions: From the output it can be observed that the Fcal>F tab (5, 20, 0.05) moreover the p-value is more than the level of significance; therefore the null hypothesis rejected which means that the effect of all the varieties is statistically significant.

Note: Randomized complete block design is special case of two way ANOVA.

The model is Yij =μ + Ti+ Bj+ eij

Another example of Two Way ANOVA

An experiment was conducted in RBD in which four feeds were given to 5 cows. Analyze the data and state your conclusions.

Feed A	Feed B	Feed C	Feed D
24	49	54	64
36	43	50	56
27	42	49	59
28	40	52	57
30	46	54	55

Perform the analysis of variance.

Analyze the Data

Solution: This can be tested through fixed effect model which can be written as:	$Y_{ij} = \mu + T_i + B_j + e_{ij}$
The null hypothesis will be	$H_0: \mu_1 = \mu_2$ vs $H_1: \mu_1 \neq \mu_2$

H_1: At least one treatment significantly differs from other

The following steps will be used

Step 1: Open Excel sheet and feed the data as given.

Step 2: Go to data menu and select Data Analysis.

Step 3: Select anova single two factor without replications tool from Data Analysis dialog box.

Step 4: Give input range in two factor without replications analysis dialog box.

Step 5: Give output range in Output options for getting output in specific range of cells

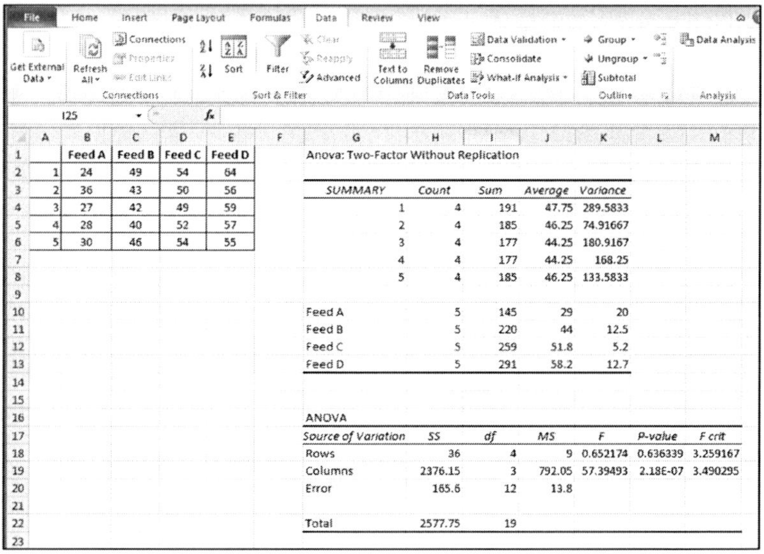

	Feed A	Feed B	Feed C	Feed D
1	24	49	54	64
2	36	43	50	56
3	27	42	49	59
4	28	40	52	57
5	30	46	54	55

Anova: Two-Factor Without Replication

SUMMARY	Count	Sum	Average	Variance
1	4	191	47.75	289.5833
2	4	185	46.25	74.91667
3	4	177	44.25	180.9167
4	4	177	44.25	168.25
5	4	185	46.25	133.5833
Feed A	5	145	29	20
Feed B	5	220	44	12.5
Feed C	5	259	51.8	5.2
Feed D	5	291	58.2	12.7

ANOVA

Source of Variation	SS	df	MS	F	P-value	F crit
Rows	36	4	9	0.652174	0.636339	3.259167
Columns	2376.15	3	792.05	57.39493	2.18E-07	3.490295
Error	165.6	12	13.8			
Total	2577.75	19				

Conclusions: From the output it can be observed that the Fcal>F tab(3, 12, 0.05) moreover the p-value is more than the level of significance; therefore the null hypothesis rejected which means that the feeds differ significantly.

Nonparametric Test

Non Parametric tests are also referred as distribution free tests. They are free of assumptions. Nonparametric tests have no assumptions regarding distribution of underlying populations or variance. Nonparametric tests are easy to perform but they are not usually as correct as parametric tests and their Null Hypotheses usually requires more evidence to be rejected than that would be in case of parametric test. Non parametric tests require little calculation. Nonparametric tests are often used when the data is ranked or ordinal or nominal. Nonparametric tests come in play when while dealing with non-numeric data, such as having rank, orders or attributes.

Sign Test

Sign test is performed when we wish to analyze two sets of the data independently and see if they are from the same sample. To perm sign test, we must have pairs of observations where the differences between observations are computed, and then determine the sign. For example, if we have collected data on two different treatments such as X and Y, the differences is computed as X-Y. if X>Y, the difference is recorded as (+) and if X<Y, it is (-).

$$Z = \frac{2R - n}{\sqrt{n}}$$

where;

R = number of positive signs,

n = number of pairs.

Problem; A poultry firm has designed a new advertising campaign to increase the sales of its eggs. To find out effectiveness of new ad campaign 14 randomly selected individual were asked to compare this new ad campaign with the old one.

Viewers	1	2	3	4	5	6	7	8	9	10	11	12	13	14
Old campaign	4	5	2	3	5	4	5	5	2	3	3	4	5	5
New campaign	3	2	4	5	1	3	4	4	2	2	3	3	4	3

To test whether this new adv. campaign is superior to old.

Solution;

Here, H_0: New Campaign > Old Campaign

H_1: New Campaign < Old Campaign

The analysis of the above data set can be obtained through the following steps.

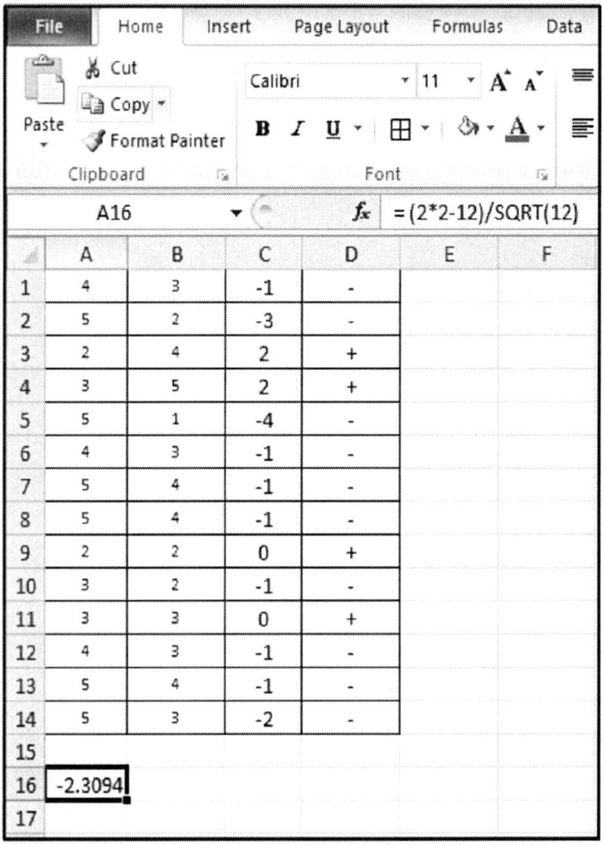

	A	B	C	D
1	4	3	-1	-
2	5	2	-3	-
3	2	4	2	+
4	3	5	2	+
5	5	1	-4	-
6	4	3	-1	-
7	5	4	-1	-
8	5	4	-1	-
9	2	2	0	+
10	3	2	-1	-
11	3	3	0	+
12	4	3	-1	-
13	5	4	-1	-
14	5	3	-2	-
15				
16	-2.3094			
17				

Step 1: Open Excel sheet and feed the data as given.

Step 2: Assign the sign according to the difference, using the difference between new campaign (X) and old campaign (Y). If old campaign (Y) is greater than new campaign then put-sign, if less then put + sign, and if there is no difference = 0.

Step 3: Type the formula Z= (2*2-12)/SQRT in the Excel sheet, then press enter in order to get the calculated Z value which is equal to -2.31

Step 4: Tabulated value of Z at=0.5 is 1.64 which is less than the calculated modulus value of Z (|Z| = |-2.31|= 2.31. So we conclude that new campaign is not superior to old.

The Wilcoxon Rank Sum Test

The Wilcoxon Rank Sum Test is counterpart of paired t - test; to determine whether there is a significant difference between the performances of two groups.

Test Procedures in Excel

Large and small sampling requires different of procedures for the Wilcoxon Rank Sum Test. The first couple steps of this test will be the same for both large and small samples. We will collect two groups of samples and then calculate the following characteristics of each group:

n_1 = Sample size of the 1st group
n_2 = Sample size of the 2nd group
N_1 = Sum of the ranks of all samples in the 1st group
N_2 = Sum of the ranks of all samples in the 2nd group
R = either N1 or N2, with the smaller sample size

First, we have to determine whether we are dealing with small samples or large samples. The small sample procedure is used if nl and n2 are both each less than 10. Use the large sample procedure if there are more than 20 samples total (nl+ n2 > 20). The small sample procedure and the large sample procedure calculate nl, n2, NI, N2, and R in the same way. Small samples and large samples use different procedures beyond this point.

Problem: An Animal breeder has formulated a new feed (X) and wishes to determine not only whether the new feed is better to the old feed (Y), but also the amount of increased weight gain. 10 animals were fed the old and new feed at two different time periods.

Feed X	0.50	0.62	0.70	0.60	0.71	0.82	0.65	0.59	0.80	0.70
Feed Y	0.56	0.60	0.72	0.65	0.68	0.85	0.68	0.71	0.91	0.64

Test difference in feeds.

Solution

H_0: The daily weight gain from two feed is same.

H_1: Daily weight gain of new feed is greater.

The analysis is as

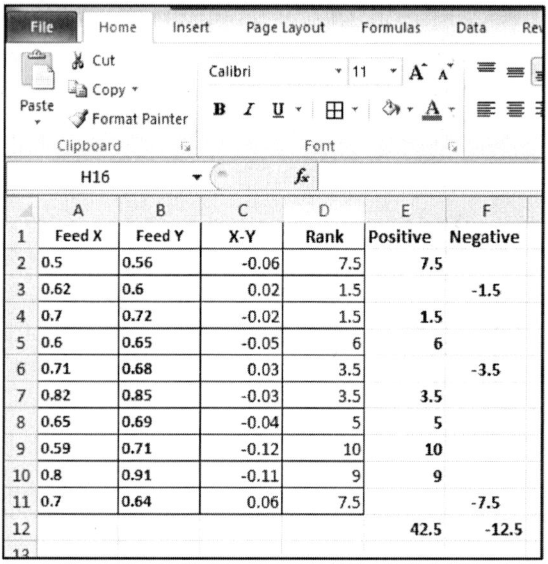

	A	B	C	D	E	F
1	Feed X	Feed Y	X-Y	Rank	Positive	Negative
2	0.5	0.56	-0.06	7.5	7.5	
3	0.62	0.6	0.02	1.5		-1.5
4	0.7	0.72	-0.02	1.5	1.5	
5	0.6	0.65	-0.05	6	6	
6	0.71	0.68	0.03	3.5		-3.5
7	0.82	0.85	-0.03	3.5	3.5	
8	0.65	0.69	-0.04	5	5	
9	0.59	0.71	-0.12	10	10	
10	0.8	0.91	-0.11	9	9	
11	0.7	0.64	0.06	7.5		-7.5
12					42.5	-12.5

Step 1: Open Excel sheet and feed the data as given.

Step 2: Determine the size and sign.

Step 3: Rank the difference irrespective of sign. Assign a rank of 1 to t smallest difference, and a high rank to the largest difference.

Step 4: Affix the appropriate signs to assigned ranks.

Step 5: Sum the ranks sum the values of positive and negative ranks. T smaller of the two sums is the Computed test statistics (T) value. Here t computed T value is -12.5. Taking the modulus value we get 12.5.

Interpretations

The computed value is compared with the table value to determine whether the null hypothesis is accepted or rejected. Given value of T at 0.05, is 10. Since the computed value is greater than the table value, we do not reject the null hypothesis, conclude that weight gain from the new feed is not different from old feed.

Mann-Whitney U Test

The Mann-Whitney U Test is a non parametric counterpart for the two-sample t-test when it can't be determined that both samples come from Normally -distributed populations. It is used to decide whether or not there is a difference between two groups or, equivalently, whether or not both groups come from the same population. Mann-Whitney test is denoted as U. The formula for this U statistics is;

$$U = n_1 n_2 + \frac{n_1 (n_1+1)}{2} - R_1$$

if $R_2 > R_1$

or

$$U = n_1 n_2 + \frac{n_2 (n_2+1)}{2} - R_2$$

if $R_2 < R_1$

Where R_1=Sum of ranks to sample 1
R_2=Sum of ranks to sample2

Problem: The data given below belongs to two groups and we have to determine if these two groups come from same populations

A	25	25	19	21	22	19	15	-	-
B	18	14	13	15	17	19	18	20	19

Test whether there is difference between A and B.

Solution

Here, H_0: A = B:

H_1: A ≠ B

The analysis of the above data set.

Step 1: Open Excel sheet and feed the data as given.

Step 2: Combine all samples into one column as shown with "A" and with "B."

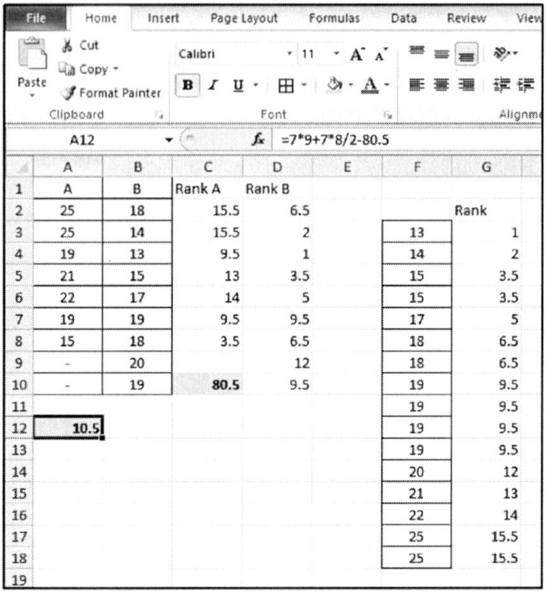

	A	B	C	D	E	F	G
1	A	B	Rank A	Rank B			
2	25	18	15.5	6.5			Rank
3	25	14	15.5	2		13	1
4	19	13	9.5	1		14	2
5	21	15	13	3.5		15	3.5
6	22	17	14	5		15	3.5
7	19	19	9.5	9.5		17	5
8	15	18	3.5	6.5		18	6.5
9	-	20		12		18	6.5
10	-	19	80.5	9.5		19	9.5
11						19	9.5
12	10.5					19	9.5
13						19	9.5
14						20	12
15						21	13
16						22	14
17						25	15.5
18						25	15.5
19							

Step 3: Rank all samples. Sort the samples by the value of each sample group and rank them in order of sample value as shown.

Step 4: Get the sum of all ranks in each group and count the ranks in each group as shown. Where N1= Count of Samples in 1st Group–7, N2 = Count of Samples in 2nd Group = 9, R1= 80.5.

Step 5: Calculate the U Statistic U = N1*N2 + [(N1 * (N1 + 1))/2] - R1 = 10.5

U = 7*9 + ((7 * (7 + 1)) /2)–80.5 = 10.5

Interpretation: Since tabulated U (7 9, .05) = 12. The calculated value of U is less that the Tabulated value. Therefore, it is concluded that there is no significant difference between the two groups.

The Kruskal-Wallis Test

The Kruskal-Wall is Test is used to know whether or not there is a difference between more than two groups or, equivalently, whether or not all groups come from the same population. This test is a non parametric counterpart for Single-Factor (One-Way) ANOVA when it cannot be determine that the samples are drawn from Normally-distributed populations. It is almost identical to the one-way (single-factor) ANOVA except that the data is replaced by the ranks of each piece of data.

The Test statistics H is calculated by using

$$H = \frac{12}{N(N+1)} \sum_{i=1}^{g} n_i \left(\bar{r}_{i\cdot} - \frac{N+1}{2} \right)^2$$
$$= \frac{12}{N(N+1)} \sum_{i=1}^{g} n_i \bar{r}_{i\cdot}^2 - 3(N+1).$$

Problem: The Data given below is based on milk yield in kgs of four different breeds of A,B,C, and D and test whether there is any significant difference between these four breeds.

A	B	C	D
4.2	3.3	1.9	3.5
4.6	2.4	2.4	3.1
3.9	2.6	2.1	3.7
4	3.8	2.7	4.1
	2.8	1.8	4.4

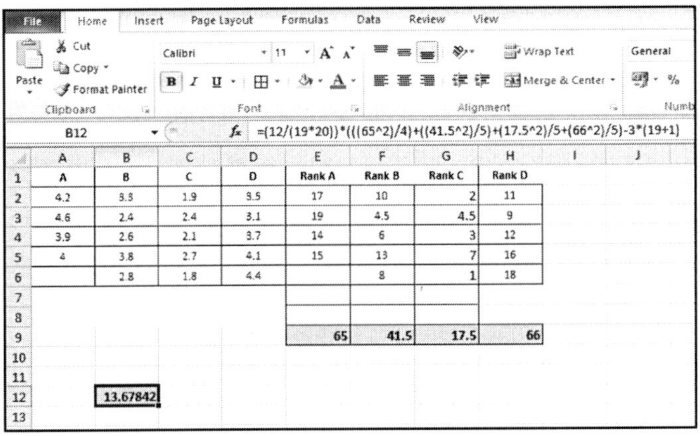

B12 f_x =(12/(19*20))*(((65^2)/4)+((41.5^2)/5)+(17.5^2)/5+(66^2)/5)-3*(19+1)

	A	B	C	D	E	F	G	H
1	A	B	C	D	Rank A	Rank B	Rank C	Rank D
2	4.2	3.3	1.9	3.5	17	10	2	11
3	4.6	2.4	2.4	3.1	19	4.5	4.5	9
4	3.9	2.6	2.1	3.7	14	6	3	12
5	4	3.8	2.7	4.1	15	13	7	16
6		2.8	1.8	4.4		8	1	18
7								
8								
9					65	41.5	17.5	66
10								
11								
12		13.67842						
13								

Solution: Here, H_0: All the breed populations are identical, H_1= otherwise the analysis of the above data

Step 1: Open Excel sheet and feed the data as given.

Step 2: Combine all four breeds into one group as shown. In

this case, each sample in the 1st group is labelled "A,". 2nd group is labelled "B," 3rd group is labelled "C" and with group as D.

Step 3: Rank observation by typing rank in Excel and Put samples back in original groups. Do this by sorting by the A B C and D.

Step 4: Get the sum of ranks of each group as shown

Step 5: Calculate the following Metrics N, = Count of Samples in 1st Group = 4, N2 = Count of Samples in 2nd Group & other is 5. Total Number of Samples = 19 k = Number of Groups = 4, df = Degrees of Freedom = k - 1 = 3

Step 6: Calculate the H Statistic by the following formula in Excel sheet in any cell in order to get H statistic = [12 / { n*(n + 1) }] * [(R1 ∧)/N1 + (R2∧N2 + (R3∧)/N3 + (R4∧)/N4]-3*(n+ 1) H Statistic = 13.678

Step 7: Calculate H Critical

H calculated as chisquare = 7.81

Excel formula:

H Critical < H Calculated

Interpretations

The, H Statistic > H Critical. So the result is statistically significant and we can state within 95% that there is significant difference between four breeds.

Chapter 6

Drawing Graphs Using Ms-Excel

Bar Graph

The following table shows the data (hypothetical) on expenditure in Rs. of a family in year 2018

Items of Expenditure (Rs)

Housing	Food and Education	Clothing
6000	10000	7000

Represent the above data by the means of Bar Graph.

Solution

Steps used for plotting the bar graph are as:

Step 1: Open Excel sheet and feed the above data as given.

Step 2: Select data and go to insert menu and select column chart.

Step 3: Select 2-D column, option first from dialog Box.

Step 4: The desired output will be as shown.

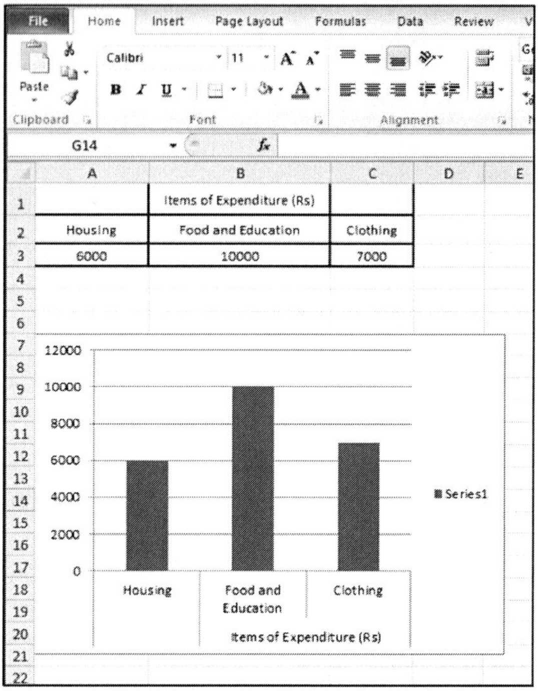

Remark The data labels, axis name, title of the graph etc. can be inserted through selecting option formatting chart area and add data labels by right clicking on the graph output.

Multiple Bar Graph

The average removal of nitrogen by weeds (kg/ha) under different weedicides in three different days after sowing (DAS) were as follows:

Weedicide	Removal of nitrogen by weeds (kg/ha)		
	30 DAYS	60 DAYS	At harvest
Oxadiazon	2.6	1.5	1.9
Fluchloralin	6.3	2.6	4.5
Isoprofuron	10.4	3.2	7.9
Unweeded Control	27.5	52.1	64.0

Draw the Multiple bar Graphs for the Above Data

Solution

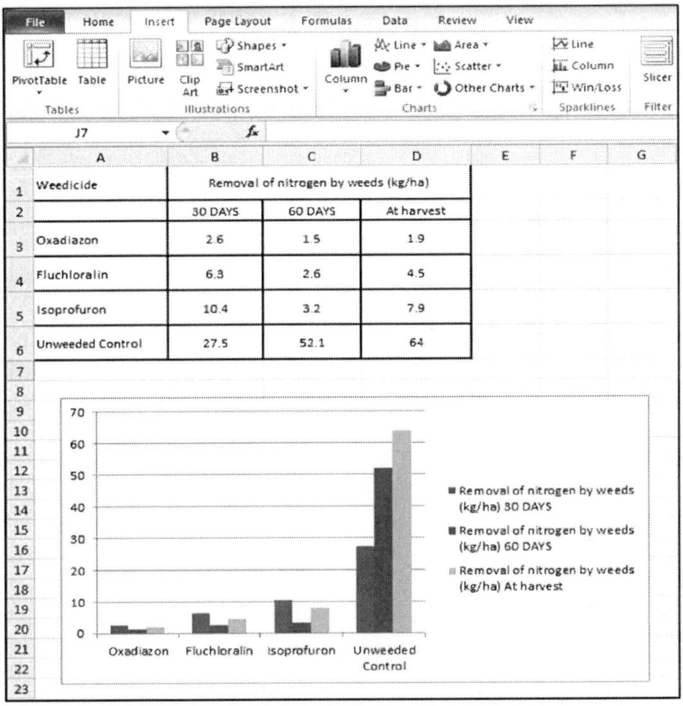

Weedicide	Removal of nitrogen by weeds (kg/ha)		
	30 DAYS	60 DAYS	At harvest
Oxadiazon	2.6	1.5	1.9
Fluchloralin	6.3	2.6	4.5
Isoprofuron	10.4	3.2	7.9
Unweeded Control	27.5	52.1	64

Step 1: Open Excel sheet and feed the above data as given in above table.

Step 2: Select data and go to insert menu and select column chart.

Step 3: Select 2-D column, option second from dialog box.

Step 4: The desired output for multiple bar graph will be displayed as shown.

Sub Divided Bar Graphs for the Above Data

Solution

Step 1: Open Excel sheet and feed the above data as given in above table.

Step 2: Select data and go to insert menu and select column chart.

Step 3: Select 2-D column, option second from dialog box.

Step 4: The desired output for sub divided bar graph will be displayed as shown.

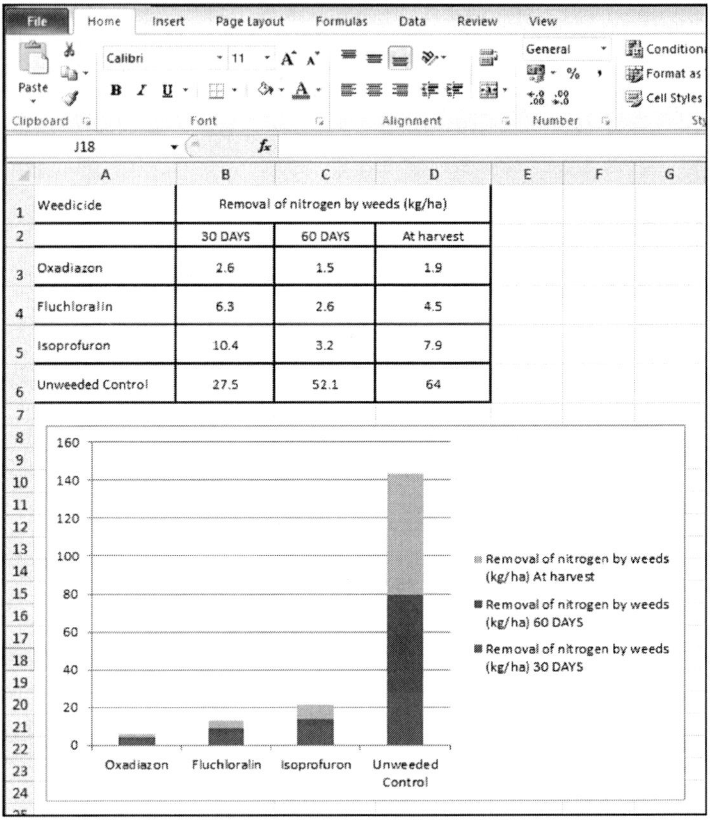

Weedicide	Removal of nitrogen by weeds (kg/ha)		
	30 DAYS	60 DAYS	At harvest
Oxadiazon	2.6	1.5	1.9
Fluchloralin	6.3	2.6	4.5
Isoprofuron	10.4	3.2	7.9
Unweeded Control	27.5	52.1	64

Pie Diagram

Draw a pie graph for the following data:

Livestock	Numbers
Cows	120
Horse	100
Hens	250
Ducks	300
Ghese	50

Solution

Steps used for plotting the pie graph are as:

Step 1: Open Excel sheet and feed the above data as given.

Step 2: Select data and go to insert menu and select pie chart.

Step 3: Select 2-D pie from dialog box.

Step 4: The desired output will be as shown.

Step 5: We can insert data labels, axis name, title of the graph etc. through selecting format data series and add data labels by right clicking on th graph output.

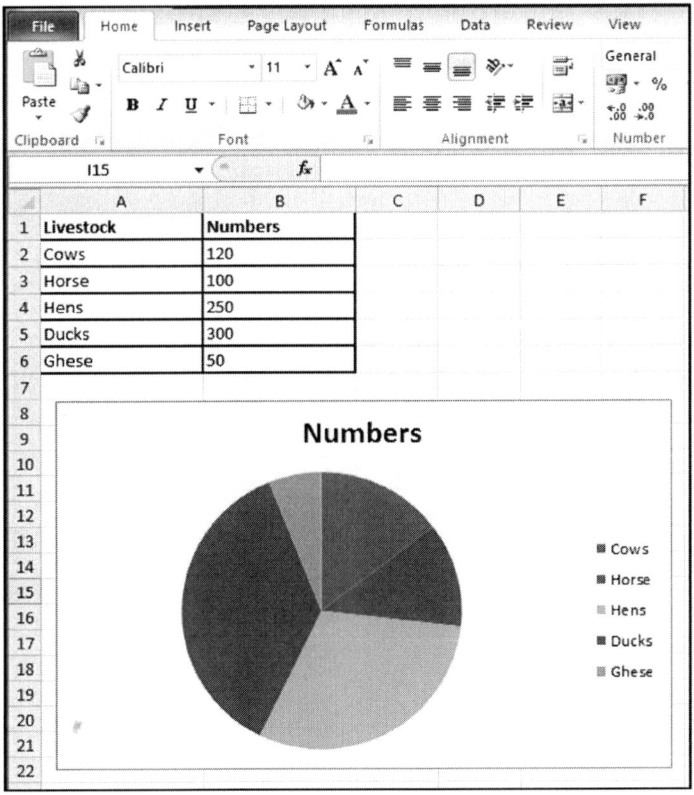

Step 6: Data labels can be formatted and value of data can be added to the pi chart.

Step 7: Select percentage from data labels dialog box.

Step 8: The desired pie chart with percentage share of each commodity as shown.

Line Diagram with One Axis

The following table gives the data (hypothetical) on expenditure in Rs. of a family in different years:

Years	Items of Expenditure (Rs)		
	Food	Clothing	Education
2000	1000	800	900
2005	1500	1200	1600
2010	2000	1800	2500
2015	3000	2800	3400

Represent the above data by the means of line chart.

Solution

Steps used for plotting the line diagram are as:

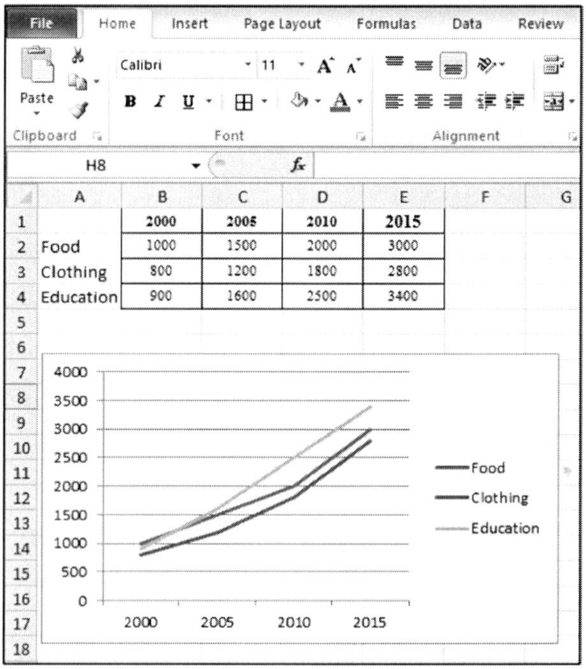

Step 1: Open Excel sheet and feed the above data as given.
Step 2: Select data and go to insert menu and select line chart.
Step 3: Select 2-D line from dialog box.
Step 4: The desired output will be as shown.

Remark: The data labels, axis name, title of the graph etc. can be inserted through selecting option formatting chart area and add data labels by right clicking on the graph output.

Line Diagram with Two Axis

The hypothetical data for monthly arrivals and prices of Potato, Onion, and Broccoli for the year 2016 - 17 is given below:

Particulars	Vegetable wise Arrivals (Tons.)			Vegetable wise Prices (/qtl.)		
	Potato	Onion	Broccoli	Potato	Onion	Broccoli
April	5546.6	2930	2641.33	3780.5	1557	3028.33
May	2833.33	2942.5	4276.8	4211	1588	2615.4
June	3469	2430	7764	4023	1591	2074.75
July	3285.5	2821	4756.4	3628	1388	1764.2
August	3716	3091.5	3350.2	2961	1698	2770.6
September	4626.67	3120	2683.8	3127.67	2177	2854.4
October	3083.4	3324	2741	2869.5	1746	2865
November	4474	3302.25	1959	2620.5	1604	2053
December	9444.4	10904	2151.8	3092.75	2092.6	1626.8
January	7834.8	7522	2651	3316.75	2263	2458.6
February	12651.4	8504	7214	3191.75	2292.2	2758.2
March	6449.4	2909	3095	3514.75	2215.2	3148.6

Plot the above data with two axes.

Solution

Step 1: Open Excel sheet and feed the above data as per the format as given.

Step 2: Select data and go to insert menu and select line chart

Step 3: Select 2-D line from dialog box.

Step 4: The output will be as shown.

Step 5: By right clicking on the graph select format data series from the dialog box.

Step 6: Check in Secondary axis from the series options from the format data series dialog box.

Step 7: The desired output with two axes related to arrivals and prices of fruits is shown.

	A	B	C	D	E	F	G
1	Particulars	Vegetable wise Arrivals (Tons.)			Vegetable wise Prices (Tons.)		
2							
3		Potato	Onion	Broccoli	Potato	Onion	Broccoli
4	April	5546.6	2930	2641.33	3780.5	1557	3028.33
5	May	2833.33	2942.5	4276.8	4211	1588	2615.4
6	June	3469	2430	7764	4023	1591	2074.75
7	July	3285.5	2821	4756.4	3628	1388	1764.2
8	August	3716	3091.5	3350.2	2961	1698	2770.6
9	September	4626.67	3120	2683.8	3127.67	2177	2854.4
10	October	3083.4	3324	2741	2869.5	1746	2865
11	November	4474	3302.25	1959	2620.5	1604	2053
12	December	9444.4	10904	2151.8	3092.75	2092.6	1626.8
13	January	7834.8	7522	2651	3316.75	2263	2458.6
14	February	12651.4	8504	7214	3191.75	2292.2	2758.2
15	March	6449.4	2909	3095	3514.75	2215.2	3148.6

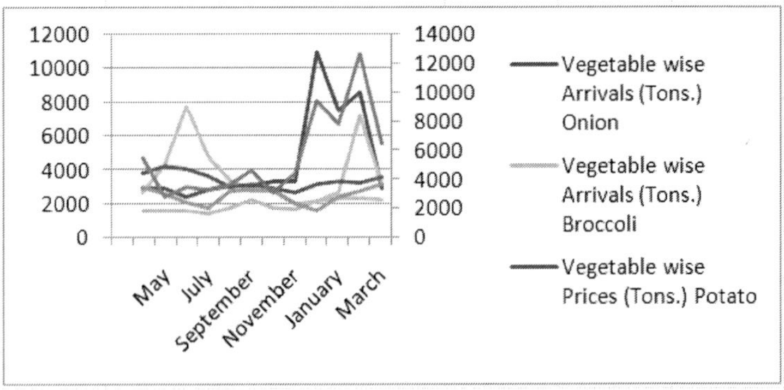

Scattered Diagram and Regression Equation

Following table gives the length of plant (in cm) and panicle length for ten plants.

Length of plant	Panicle Length
22.9	112
23.9	131
24.8	147
21.2	90
22.2	110
22.7	106
23	127
24	145
20.6	85
21	95
24	142
23.1	111

Draw a scattered graph and also calculate the linear regression equation of panicle length of plant through scattered diagram.

Solution

Steps used for plotting the scattered graph are as:

Step 1: Open Excel sheet and feed the above data as given.

Step 2: Select data and go to Insert menu and select scatter from dialog box.

Step 3: Desired output of panicle length will be shown.

Step 4: Right click on the scatter points in figure select add trend line from the dialog box.

Step 5: Select linear in the trend line options.

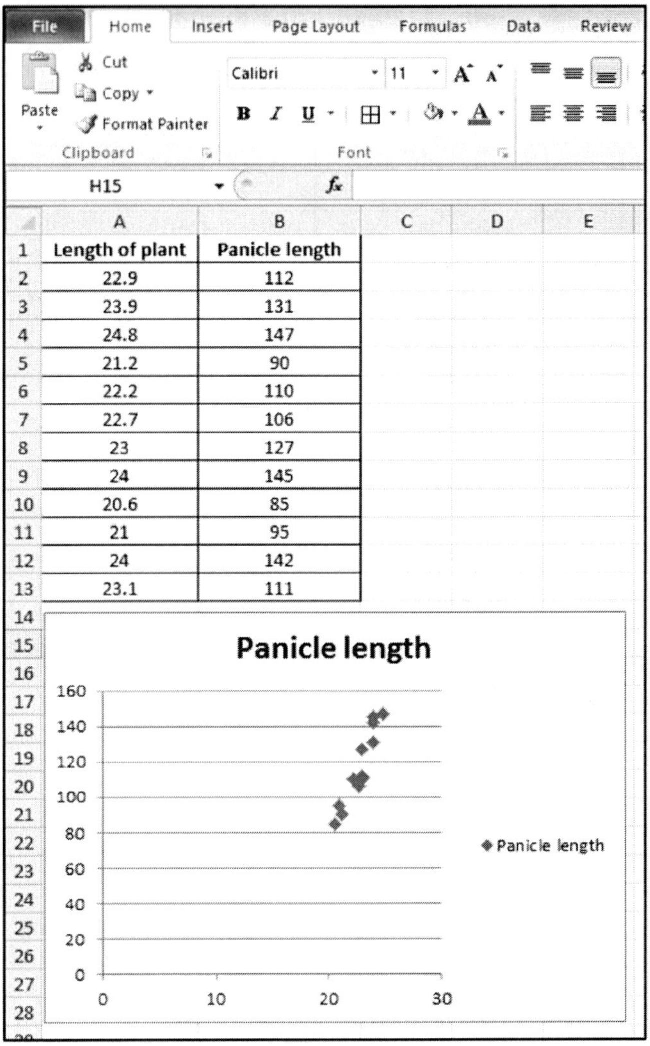

	A	B
1	Length of plant	Panicle length
2	22.9	112
3	23.9	131
4	24.8	147
5	21.2	90
6	22.2	110
7	22.7	106
8	23	127
9	24	145
10	20.6	85
11	21	95
12	24	142
13	23.1	111

Chapter 7

Flow Charts

Meaning and Definition

A flowchart is a graphical representation of decisions and the results of those decisions mapped out in individual shapes that were developed by Herman Goldstine and John von Neumann in the 1940's. Flowcharts allow for a step-by-step diagram to be drawn out that help to describe complex situations such as the steps in programming or trouble shooting a computer.

Meaning of Symbols

Terminal points or starting point: represents the beginning of flowchart.

Process box: Process represents a step in your process

The input/action symbol represents a user response that directs the course flow from that point onwards, i.e., an online test or questionnaire form.

Decision Box: indicates a point where the outcome of a decision dictates the next step. There can be multiple outcomes, but often there are just two - yes and no.

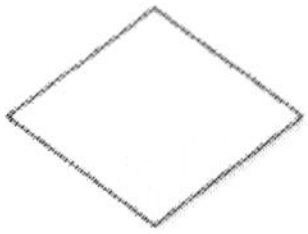

Data shape: indicates that information is coming into the process from outside, or leaving the process.

Database shape: Use this shape for a step that results in information being stored.

Document represents a step that results in a document or print statement.

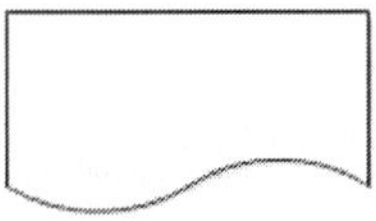

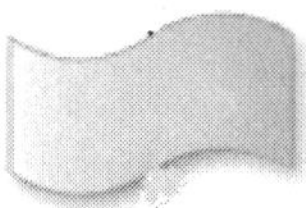

Types of Flowchart

1. **System Flowchart:** A flowchart showing the process of working on a system. But do not drill down into sub-systems.

2. **Program Flowchart:** Flowchart shows the steps in the program. From the data calculated to show the results.

General Rules for Flowcharting

1. All boxes of the flowchart are connected with Arrows. (Not lines)
2. Flowchart symbols have an entry point on the top of the symbol with no other entry points. The exit point for all flowchart symbols is on the bottom except for the Decision symbol.
3. The Decision symbol has two exit points; these can be on the sides or the bottom and one side.
4. Generally a flowchart will flow from top to bottom. However, an upward flow can also be shown.
5. Connectors are used to connect breaks in the flowchart. Examples are:
   - From one page to another page.
   - From the bottom of the page to the top of the same page.
   - An upward flow of more than 3 symbols
6. Subroutines and Interrupt programs have their own and independent flowcharts.
7. All flow charts start with a Terminal or Predefined Process (for interrupt programs or subroutines) symbol.
8. All flowcharts end with a terminal or a contentious loop.

Advantages of Flowchart

1. Conveys Better Meaning

Since a flowchart is a pictorial representation of a program, it is easier for a programmer to understand and explain the logic of the program to other programmers.

2. Analyses the Problem Effectively

Flow chart helps the programmers to analyze the problem in detail by breaking the flow chart into detailed parts.

3. Effective Coding

It is very easy for the programmers to write the program, because flow chart will give a clear idea of the steps involved.

4. Systematic Debugging

Even after taking the full care in program design, some errors may remain in the program because the programmer might have never thought of a particular case. Using a flow chart can reduce this type of errors. It also enables easy detection of errors.

Advantages of Using Flowcharts

As we discussed flow chart is used for representing algorithm in pictorial form. This pictorial representation of a solution/system is having many advantages. These advantages are as follows:

1. *Communication:* A Flowchart can be used as a better way of communication of the logic of a system and steps involve in the solution, to all concerned particularly to the client of system.
2. *Effective analysis:* A flowchart of a problem can be used for effective analysis of the problem.
3. *Documentation of Program/System:* Program flowcharts are a vital part of a good program documentation. Program document is used for various purposes like knowing the components in the program, complexity of the program etc.
4. *Efficient Program Maintenance:* Once a program is developed and becomes operational it needs time to time maintenance. With help of flowchart maintenance become easier.
5. *Coding of the Program:* Any design of solution of a problem is finally converted into computer program. Writing code referring the flowchart of the solution become easy.

The Three Basic Control Structures

Our programs are made up of the three basic constructers of: sequence, selection, and repetition.

1. Sequence

The sequence control structure is defined as the straight forward execution of one processing step after another. Here is the general form of a sequence.

2. Selection (Decision)

The selection control structure can be defined as the presentation of a condition, and the choice between two actions depending on whether the condition is true or false. Here is the general form of the selection construct.

3: Repetition (Iteration or Looping)

The repetition control structure can be defined as the presentation of a set of instructions to be performed recently, as long as a condition is true. Here is the general form of repetition.

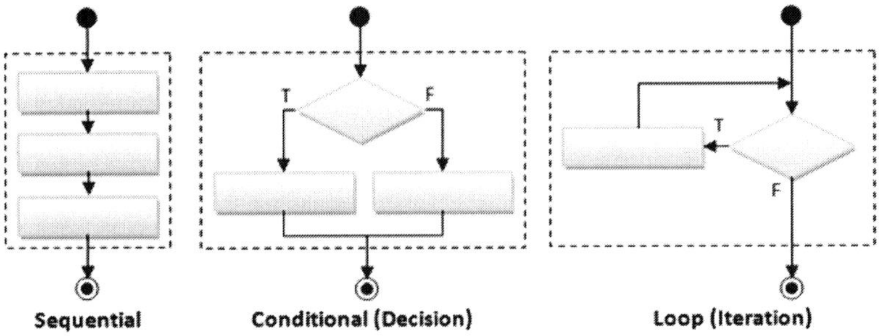

Algorithm and Flowchart for Solving Problem

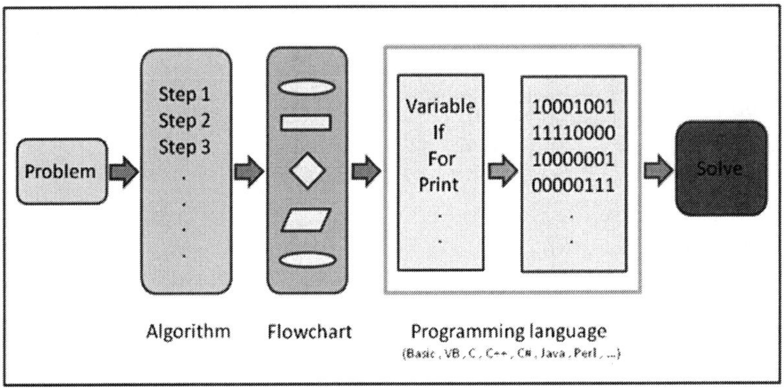

Illustrations Through Examples

1. Algorithm and flow chart to read the name and print the name.

Algorithm Flow Chart	Flow Chart
Step 1: Start Step 2: Read input name Step 3: Print name Step 4: Stop	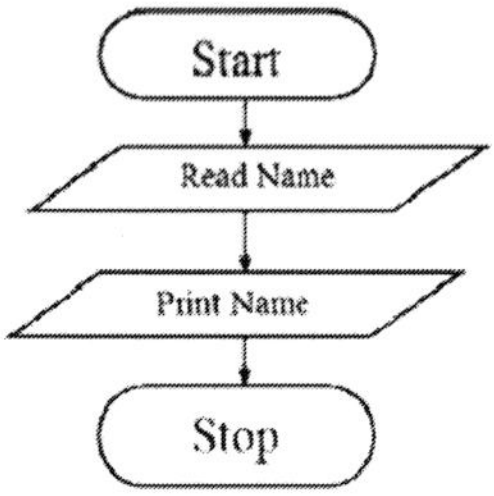

2. Algorithm and flow chart to add two numbers.

Algorithm Flow Chart	Flow Chart
Step 1: Start Step 2: Input first number A Step 3: Input second number B Step 4: Add the two numbers and store it in total Step 5: Print Total Step 6: Stop	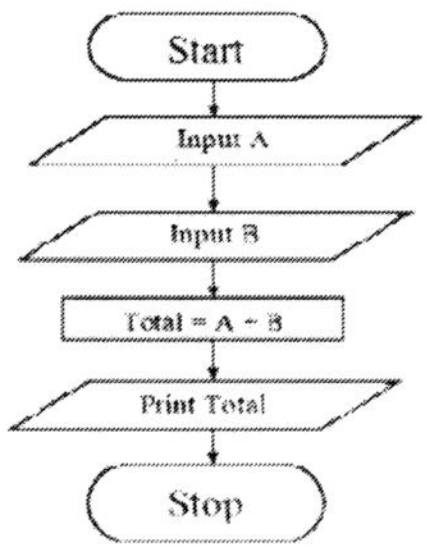

3. Algorithm and a flow chart to calculate area of square.

Algorithm Flow Chart	Flow Chart
Step 1 : Start Step 2 : Read value for a (side) Step 3 : [Compute] Area = A * A Step 4 : Print Area Step 5 : Stop	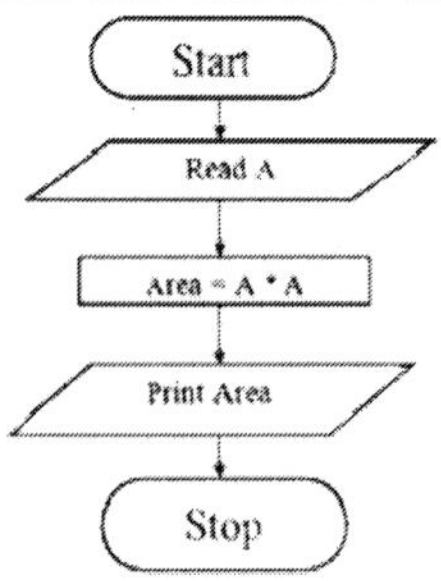

4. Algorithm and flow chart to find the average of three numbers.

Algorithm Flow Chart

Step 1 : Start

Step 2 : Enter Three Numbers A, Band C

Step 3 : Compute Average = (A+B+C)/3

Step 4 : Print Average

Step 5 : Stop

Flow Chart

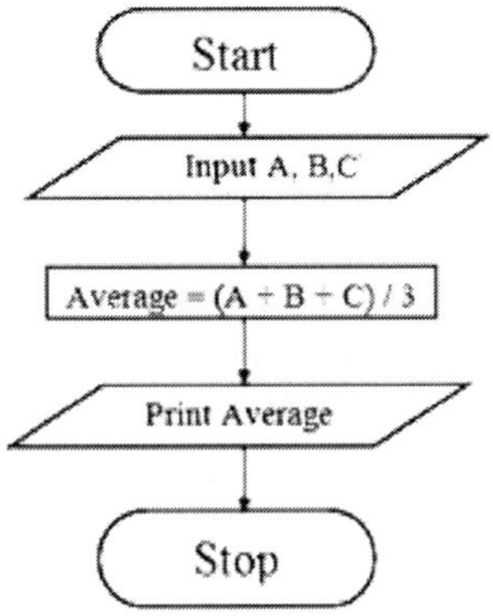

5. Algorithm and flow chart to find the largest of two numbers.

Algorithm Flow Chart

Step 1: Start

Step 2: Enter two numbers A and B

Step 3: Check if A is greater than B if yes go to Step 4 else go to Step 5

Step 4: Print A is greater than B

Step 5: Check if B is greater than A if yes go to Step 6 else go to Step 7

Step 6: Print B is greater than A

Step 7: Print A is equal to B

Step 8: Stop

Flow Chart

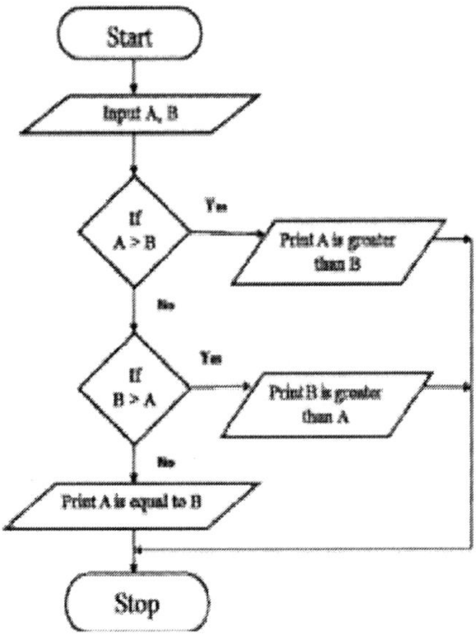

6. Algorithm and a flow chart to find the factorial of a number

Algorithm Flow Chart	Flow Chart
Step 1: Start Step 2: Read N Step 3: [Initialize all counters] Set FACT= 1, i = 1 Step 4: Compute Fact = Fact * I Increment i Step 5: Check if i< = N if true repeat step 4 if false go to step 6 Step 6: Print fact Step 7: Stop	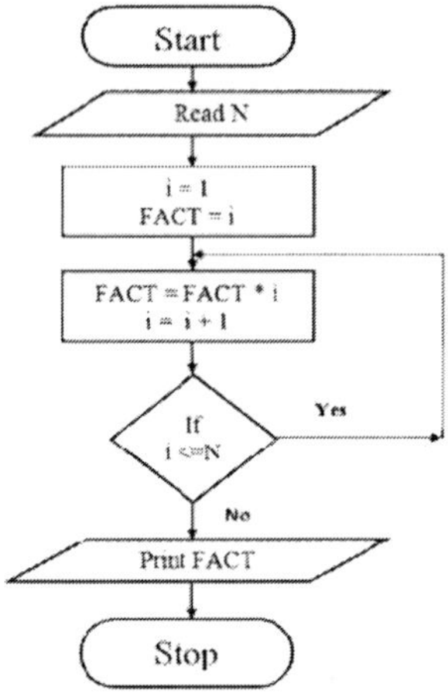

7. Calculate and print the average of three numbers: 5, 10, and 15.

Algorithm Flow Chart	Flow Chart
Step 1: Start Step 2: num1 = 5 Step 3: num2 = 10 Step 4: num3 = 15 Step 5: sum = num1 + num2 + num3 Step 6: average = sum/3.0 Step 7: print average Step 8: Stop	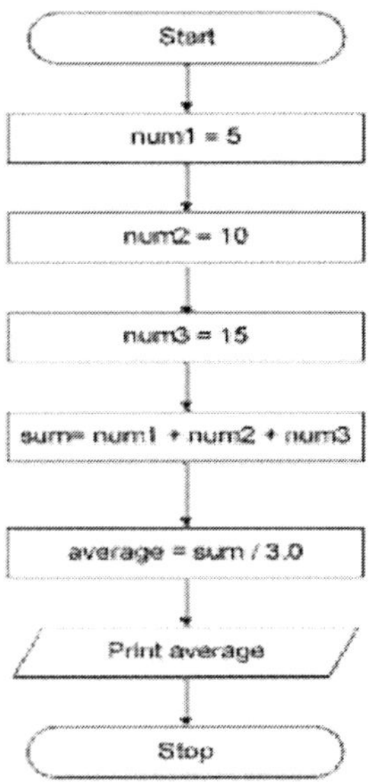

Draw a Flowchart, which will Calculate Greatest Milk Yield Among Three Cows Represented by A, B & C?

Sol.

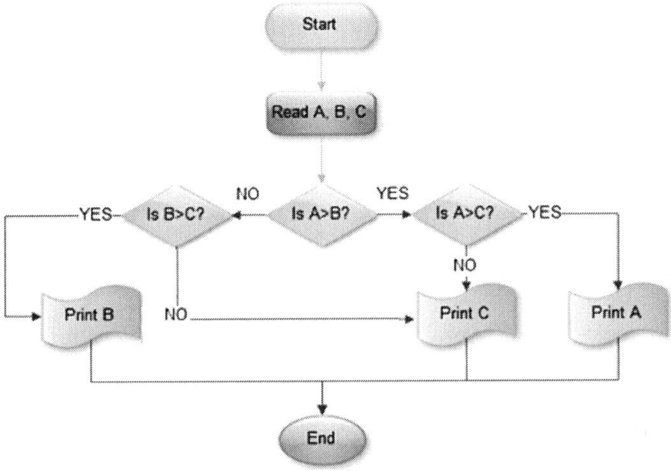

Write a program for above flowchart in 'C' Language?

Sol

```
main()
{
  int A, B, C;
  clrscr( );
  printf("Enter Data for A B C\n");
  scanf("%d %d %d", &A, &B, &C);
  if ( A > B )
  if ( A > C )
  printf ("Milk Yield of Cow A is greater = %d\n", A ); else
  printf("Milk Yield of Cow C is greater = %d\n", C); else
  if ( B > C )
  printf ("Milk Yield of Cow B is greater = %d\n", B ); else
  printf ("Milk Yield of Cow C is greater = %d\n", C ); }
```

Write a 'C' program to calculate the Mean, Variance & Standard Deviation of data.

```
#include <stdio.h>
#include <math.h>
#define MAXSIZE 10
void main()
{
float x [MAXSIZE]; /* x array contains elements */ inti, n;
float average, variance, std_deviation, sum = 0, sum1 = 0;
clrscr( );
printf("Enter the value of N \n");
scanf("%d", &n);
printf("Enter %d real numbers \n", n);
for (i = 0; i< n; i++) /* Loop till all elements are obtained*/
scanf("%f", &x[i] );
for (i = 0; i< n; i++) /* Compute the sum of all elements */
sum = sum + x[i];
average = sum / (float)n;
for (i = 0; i< n; i++) /* Compute variance and standard
deviation */
sum1 = sum1 + pow( (x[i] - average) , 2 );
variance = sum1 / (float)n;
std_deviation = sqrt(variance);
printf("Average of all elements = %.2f\n", average);
printf("variance of all elements = %.2f\n", variance);
printf("Standard deviation = %.2f\n", std_deviation);
}
```

Chapter 8

Introduction to Database Management System

Here we confine ourself to one of the Database Management System (DBMS) i.e. Ms-Access from Microsoft that combines the relational Microsoft Jet Database Engine with a graphical user interface and software development tools. It is a member of the Microsoft Office suite of applications, included in the professional and higher editions. Microsoft Access is just one part of Microsoft's overall data management product strategy. It stores data in its own format based on the Access Jet Database Engine.

Like relational databases, Microsoft Access also allows you to link related information easily. It can also import or link directly to data stored in other applications and databases.

As its name implies, Access can work directly with data from other sources, including many popular PC database programs, with many SQL (Structured Query Language) databases on the desktop, on servers, on minicomputers, or on mainframes, and with data stored on Internet or intranet web servers.

Access can also understand and use a wide variety of other data formats, including many other database file structures. You can export data to and import data from word processing files, spreadsheets, or database files directly. Access can work with most popular databases that support the Open Database Connectivity (ODBC) standard, including SQL Server, Oracle, and DB2.

Software developers can use Microsoft Access to develop application software. Microsoft Access stores information which is called a database. To use MS Access, you will need to follow these four steps -

Database Creation - Create your Microsoft Access database and specify what kind of data you will be storing.

Data Input - After your database is created, the data of every business day can be entered into the Access database.

Query - This is a fancy term to basically describe the process of retrieving information from the database.

Report (optional) - Information from the database is organized in a nice presentation that can be printed in an Access Report.

Architecture

Access calls anything that can have a name an object. Within an Access desktop database, the main objects are tables, queries, forms, reports, macros, data macros, and modules. If you have worked with other database systems on desktop computers, you might have seen the term database used to refer to only those files in which you store data. But, in Access, a desktop database (.accdb) also includes all the major objects related to the stored data, including objects you define to automate the use of your data. Microsoft Access has the look and feel of other Microsoft Office products as far as its layout and navigational aspects are concerned, but MS Access is a database and, more specifically, a relational database.

Before MS Access 2007, the file extension was *.mdb, but in MS Access 2007 the extension has been changed to *.accdb extension. Early versions of Access cannot read accdb extensions but MS Access 2007 and later versions can read and change earlier versions of Access. An Access desktop database (.accdb or .mdb) is a fully functional RDBMS. It provides all the data definition, data manipulation, and data control features that you need to manage large volumes of data. You can use an Access desktop database (.accdb or .mdb) either as a standalone RDBMS on a single workstation or in a shared client/server mode across a network. A desktop database can also act as the data source for data displayed on webpages on your company intranet. When you build an application with an Access desktop database, Access is the RDBMS.

Data Definition

In document or a spreadsheet, you generally have complete freedom to define the contents of the document or each cell in the spreadsheet. In a document, you can include paragraphs of text, a table, a chart, or multiple columns of data displayed with multiple fonts. In spreadsheet, you can have text data at the top to define a column header for printing or display, and you might have various numeric formats within the same column, depending on the function of the row.

An RDBMS allows you to define the kind of data you have and how the data should be stored. You can also usually define rules that the RDBMS can use to ensure the integrity of your data. For example, a validation rule might ensure that the user can't accidentally store alphabetic characters in a field that should contain a number.

Data Manipulation

Working with data in RDBMS is very different from working with data in a word processing or spreadsheet program. In a word processing document, you can include tabular data and perform a limited set of functions on the data in the document. You can also search for text strings in the original document and, with ActiveX controls, include tables, charts, or pictures from other applications. In a spreadsheet, some cells contain functions that determine the result you want, and in other cells, you enter the data that provides the source information for the functions. An RDBMS provides you many ways to work with your data. For example, you can search a single table for information or request a complex search across several related tables. You can update a single field or many records with a single command. You can write programs that use RDBMS commands to fetch data that you want to display and allow the user to update the data.

Access uses the powerful SQL database language to process data in your tables. Using SQL, you can define the set of information that you need to solve a particular problem, including data from perhaps many tables.

Data Control

Spreadsheets and word processing documents are great for solving single-user problems, but they are difficult to use when more than one person needs to share the data. When you need to share your information with others, RDBMS gives you the flexibility to allow multiple users to read or update your data. An RDBMS that is designed to allow data sharing also provides features to ensure that no two people can change the same data at the same time. The best systems also allow you to group changes so that either all the changes or none of the changes appear in your data. You might also want to be sure that no one else can view any part of the order until you have entered all of it. Because you can share your Access data with other users, you might need to set some restrictions on what various users are allowed to see or update.

MS Access uses "objects" to help the user list and organize information, as well as prepare specially designed reports. When you create a database, Access offers you Tables, Queries, Forms, Reports, Macros, and Modules. Databases in Access are composed of many objects but the following are the major objects.

- Tables
- Queries
- Forms
- Reports

Together, these objects allow you to enter, store, analyze, and compile your data. Here is a summary of the major objects in an Access database;

Table

Table is an object that is used to define and store data. When you create a new table, Access asks you to define fields which is also known as column headings. Each field must have a unique name, and data type. Tables contain fields or columns that store different kinds of data, such as a name or an address, and records or rows that collect all the information about a particular instance of the subject, such as all the information about a customer or employee etc. You can define a primary key, one or more fields that have a unique value for each record, and one or more indexes on each table to help retrieve your data more quickly.

Query

An object that provides a custom view of data from one or more tables. Queries are a way of searching for and compiling data from one or more tables. Running a query is like asking a detailed question of your database. When you build a query in Access, you are defining specific search conditions to find exactly the data you want. In Access, you can use the graphical query by example facility or you can write Structured Query Language (SQL) statements to create your queries. You can define queries to Select, Update, Insert, or Delete data. You can also define queries that create new tables from data in one or more existing tables.

Form

Form is an object in a desktop database designed primarily for data input or display or for control of application execution. You use forms to customize the presentation of data that your application extracts from queries or tables. Forms are used for entering, modifying, and viewing records. The reason forms are used so often is that they are an easy way to guide people toward entering data correctly. When you enter information into a form in Access, the data goes exactly where the database designer wants it to go in one or more related tables.

Report

Report is an object in databases designed for formatting, calculating, printing, and summarizing selected data. You can view a report on your screen before you print it. If forms are for input purposes, then reports are for output. Anything you plan to print deserves a report, whether it is a list of names and addresses, a financial summary for a period, or a set of mailing labels. Reports are useful because they allow you to present components of your database in an easy-to-read format. You can even customize a report's appearance to make it visually appealing. Access offers you the ability to create a report from any table or query.

Module

Module is an object in desktop databases containing custom procedures that you code using Visual Basic. Modules provide a more discrete flow of actions and allow you to trap errors. Everything that can be done in a macro can also be done in a module, but you don't get the macro interface that prompts you what is needed for each action. Modules are far more powerful, and are essential if you plan to write code for a multi-user environment, because macros cannot include error handling. Modules can be standalone objects containing functions that can be called from anywhere in your application, or they can be directly associated with a form or a report to respond to events on the associated form or report.

How to Create Database

To create a database from a template, we first need to open MS Access and you will see the following screen in which different Access database templates are displayed.

Create Blank Database

Sometimes database requirements can be so specific that using and modifying the existing templates requires more work than just creating a database from scratch. In such case, we make use of blank database.

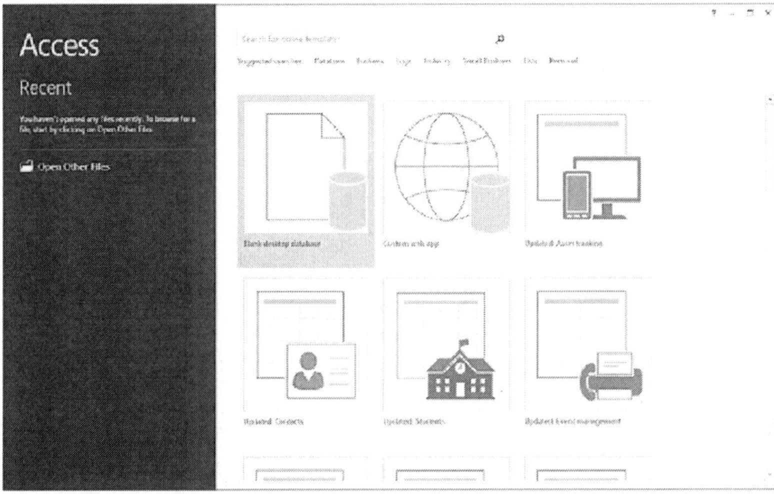

Step 1 - Let us now start by opening MS Access.

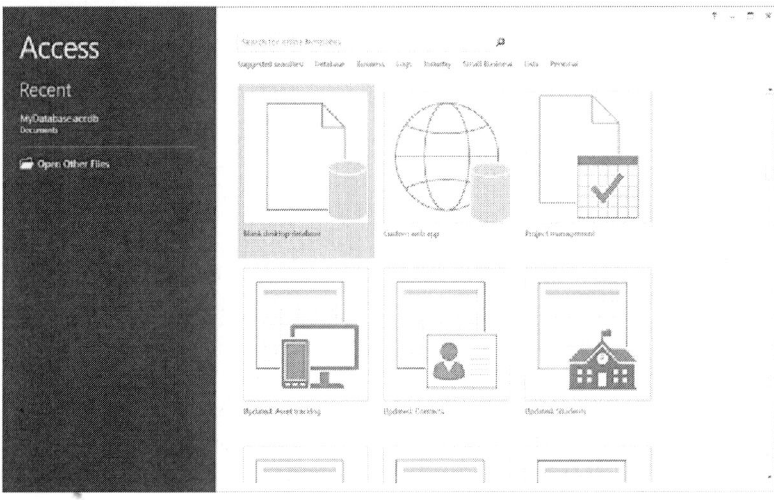

Step 2 - Select Blank desktop database. Enter the name and click the Create button.

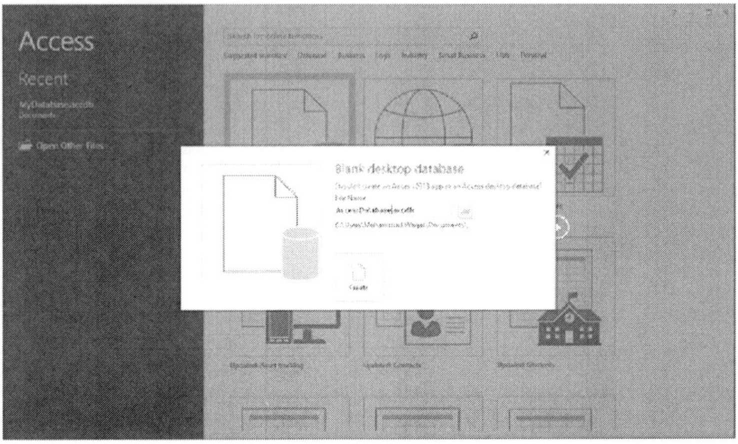

Step 3 - Access will create a new blank database and will open up the table which is also completely blank.

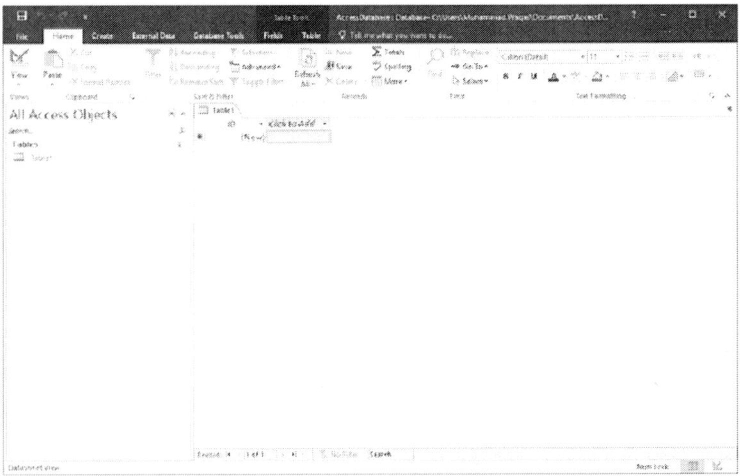

Data Types in MS Access

Every field in a table has properties and these properties define the field's characteristics and behavior. The most important property for a field is its data type. A field's data type determines what kind of data it can store. MS Access supports different types of data, each with a specific purpose. The data type determines the kind of the values that users can store in any given field. Each field can store data consisting of only a single data type. Here are some of the most common data types you will find used in a typical Microsoft Access database.

Type of Data	Description	Size
Number	Numeric data used in mathematical calculations.	1, 2, 4, or 8 bytes (16 bytes if set to Replication ID).
Date/Time	Date and time values for the years 100 through 9999.	8 bytes
Currency	Currency values and numeric data used in mathematical calculations involving data with one to four decimal places.	8 bytes
AutoNumber	A unique sequential (incremented by 1) number or random number assigned by Microsoft Access whenever a new record is added to a table.	4 bytes (16 bytes if set to Replication ID).
Attachment	Files, such as digital photos. Multiple files can be attached per record. This data type is not available in earlier versions of Access.	Up to about 2 GB.
OLE objects	OLE objects can store pictures, audio, video, or other BLOBs (Binary Large Objects)	Up to about 2 GB.
Hyperlink	Text or combinations of text and numbers stored as text and used as a hyperlink address.	Up to 8,192 (each part of a Hyperlink data type can contain up to 2048 characters).

MS Access - Create Tables: -

When you create a database, you store your data in tables, you should always start your design of a database by creating all of its tables and then creating any other object. Before you create tables, carefully consider your requirements and determine all the tables that you need. Let us try and create the first table that will store the basic contact information concerning the employees as shown in the following table –

Field Name	Data Type
EmployeeID	AutoNumber
FirstName	Text
LastName	Text
Address1	Text
Address2	Text
City	Text
State	Text
Zip	Text
Phone	Text
Phone Type	Text

Let us now have *"Text"* as the data type for all these fields and open a blank database in Access.

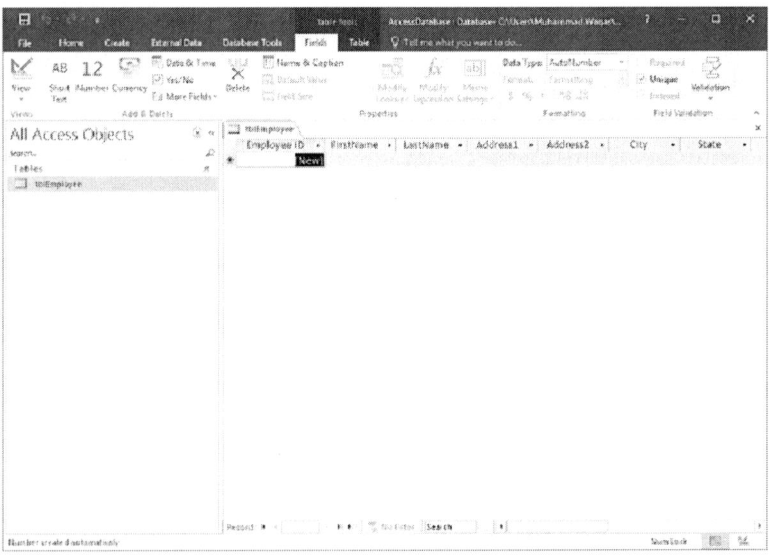

Now Adding Data

An Access database is not a file in the same sense as a Microsoft Office Word document or a Microsoft Office PowerPoint are. Instead, an Access database is a collection of objects like tables, forms, reports, queries etc. that must work together for a database to function properly. We have now created two tables with all of the fields and field properties necessary in our database. To view, change, insert, or delete data in a table within Access, you can use the table's Datasheet View. A datasheet is a simple way to look at your data in rows and columns without any special formatting. Whenever you create a new web table, Access automatically creates two views that you can start using immediately for data entry. A table open in Datasheet View resembles an Excel worksheet, and you can type or paste data into one or more fields. You do not need to explicitly save your data. Access commits your changes to the table when you move the cursor to a new field in the same row, or when you move the cursor to another row.

By default, the fields in an Access database are set to accept a specific type of data, such as text or numbers. You must enter the type of data that the field is set to accept. If you don't, Access displays an error message.

Let us add some data into your tables by opening the Access database we have created.

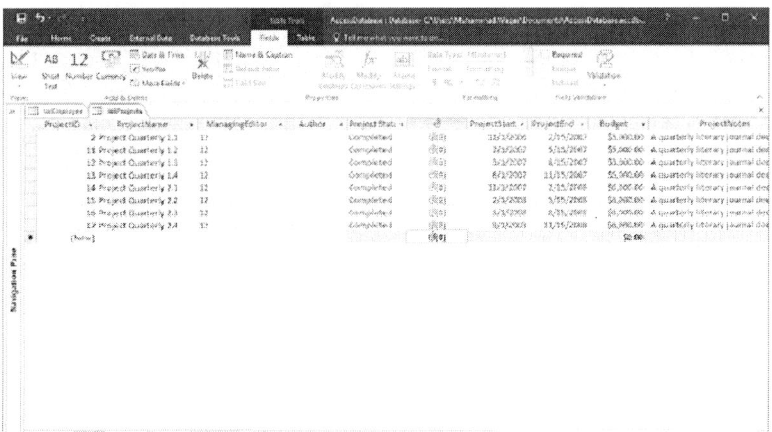

You can now see that inserting a new data and updating the existing data is very simple in Datasheet View as working in spreadsheet. But if you want to delete any data you need to select the entire row first as shown in the following screenshot. Now press the delete button. This will display the confirmation message. Click **Yes** and you will see that the selected record is deleted now.

Query in Access

Query criteria helps you to retrieve specific items from an Access database. If an item matches with all the criteria you enter, it appears in the query results. When you want to limit the results of a query based on the values in a field, you use query criteria.

- A query criterion is an expression that Access compares to query field values to determine whether to include the record that contains each value.
- Some criteria are simple, and use basic operators and constants. Others are complex, and use functions, special operators, and include field references.
- To add some criteria to a query, you must open the query in the Design View.
- You then identify the fields for which you want to specify criteria.

Example

Let's look at a simple example in which we will use criteria in a query. First open your Access database and then go to the Create tab and click on Query Design.

In the Tables tab on Show Table dialog, double-click on the **tblEmployees** table and then close the dialog box.

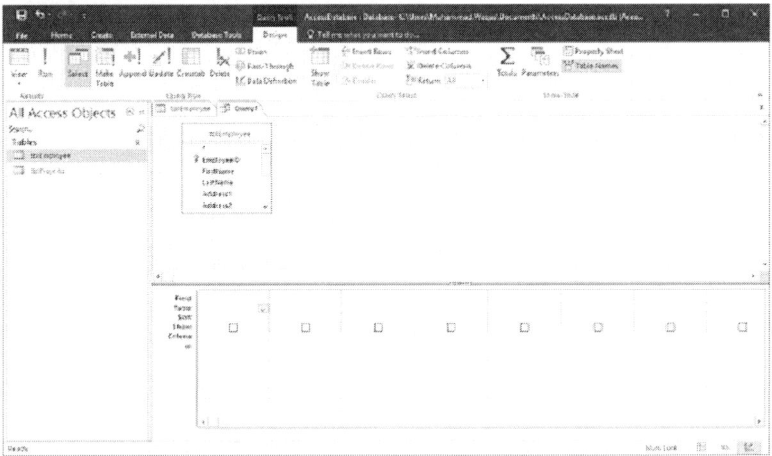

Let us now add some field to the query grid such as EmployeeID, FirstName, LastName, JobTitle and Email as shown in the following screenshot.

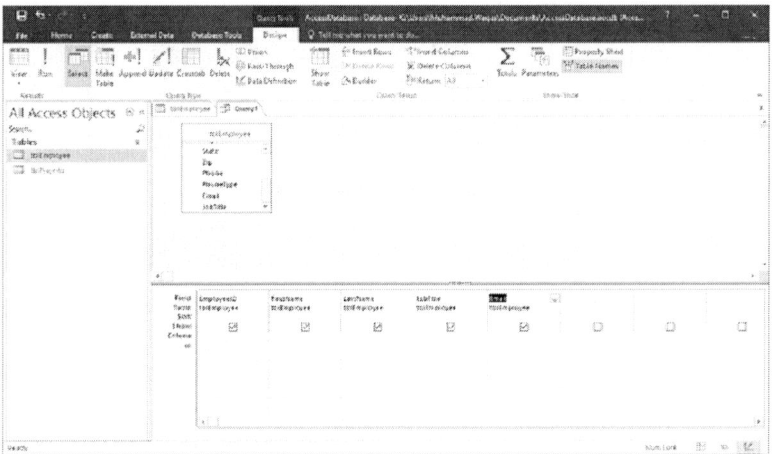

Let us now run your query and you will see only these fields as query result.

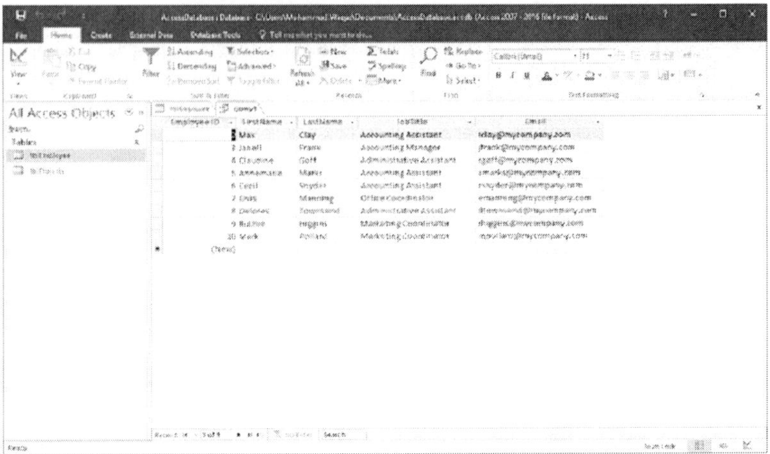

If you want to see only those whose JobTitle are Marketing Coordinator, then you will need to add the criteria for that. Let's go to the Query Design again and in Criteria row of JobTitle enter Marketing Coordinator.

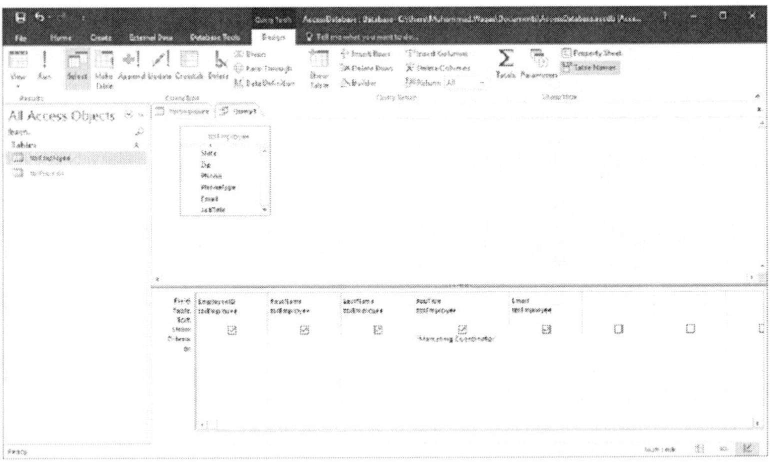

Let us now run your query again and you will see that only Job title of Marketing Coordinators are retrieved.

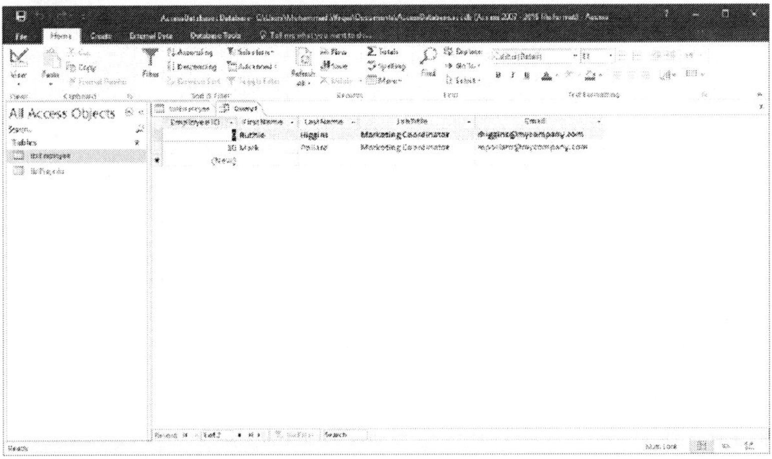

If you want to add criteria for multiple fields, just add the criteria in multiple fields. Let us say we want to retrieve data only for "Marketing Coordinator" and "Accounting Assistant"; we can specify the OR row operator as shown in the following screenshot –

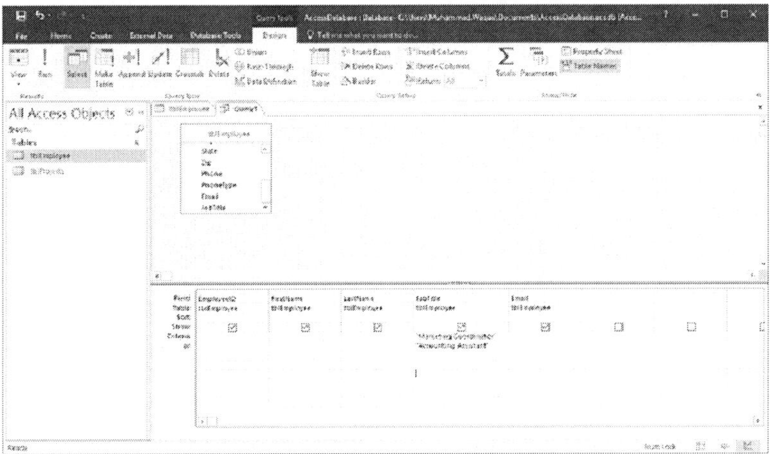

Let us now run your query again and you will see the following results.

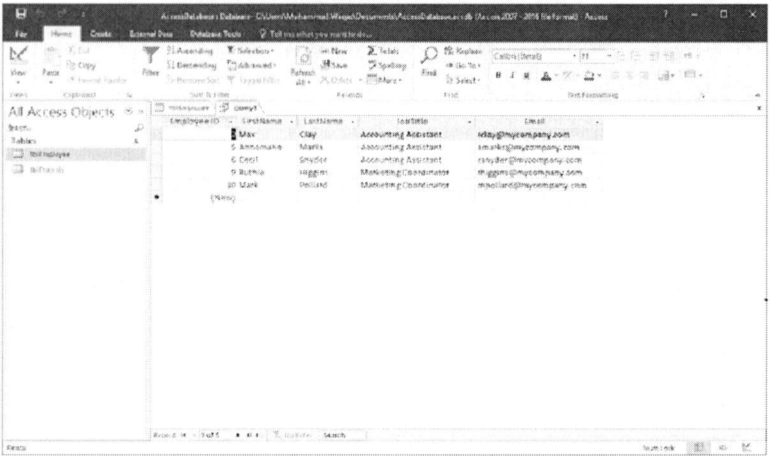

If you need to use the functionality of the **AND** operator, then you have to specify the other condition in the Criteria row. Let us say we want to retrieve all Accounting Assistants but only those Marketing Coordinator titles with "Pollard" as last name.

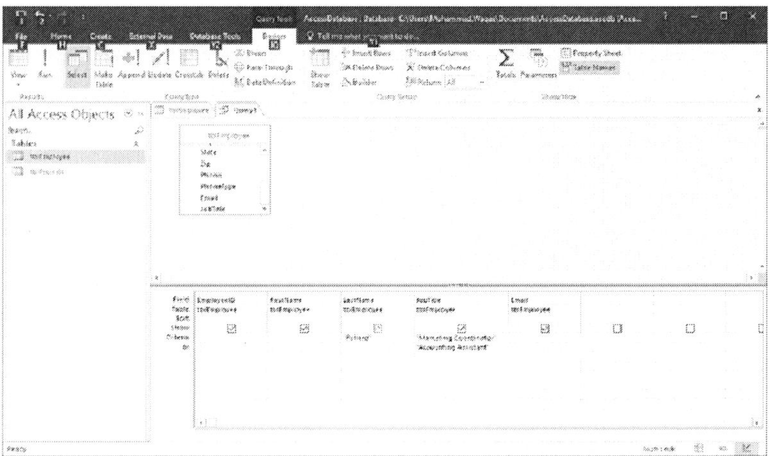

Let us now run your query again and you will see the following results.

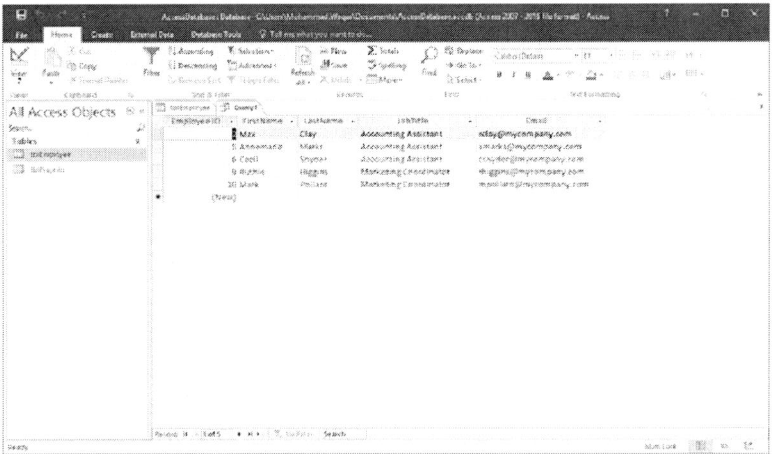

In MS Access and other DBMS systems, queries can do a lot more than just displaying data, but they can actually perform various actions on the data in your database.

- Action queries are queries that can add, change, or delete multiple records at one time.
- The added benefit is that you can preview the query results in Access before you run it.
- Microsoft Access provides 4 different types of Action Queries –
    - Append
    - Update
    - Delete
    - Make-table
- An action query cannot be undone. You should consider making a backup of any tables that you will update by using an update query.

Chapter 9

Internet Tools and Techniques

Internet refers to network of networks. In this network each computer is recognized by a globally unique address known as IP address. A special computer DNS (Domain Name Server) is used to give name to the IP Address so that user can locate a computer by a name.

For example, a DNS server will resolve a name **http://www.starvetcol.ac.in** to a particular IP address to uniquely identify the computer on which this website is hosted.

Internet is defined as an Information Super Highway, to access information over the web.

- Internet is a world-wide global system of interconnected computer networks.
- Internet uses the standard Internet Protocol (TCP/IP).
- Every computer in internet is identified by a unique IP address.
- IP Address is a unique set of numbers (such as 110.22.33.114) which identifies a computer location.
- A special computer DNS (Domain Name Server) is used to give name to the IP Address so that user can locate a computer by a name.

- For example, a DNS server will resolve a name **http://www.starvetcol.ac.in** to a particular IP address to uniquely identify the computer on which this website is hosted.
- Internet is accessible to every user all over the world.

Evolution

The concept of Internet was originated in 1969 and has undergone several technological & Infrastructural changes as discussed below:

- The origin of Internet devised from the concept of **Advanced Research Project Agency Network (ARPANET).**
- **ARPANET** was developed by United States Department of Defense.
- Basic purpose of ARPANET was to provide communication among the various bodies of government.
- Initially, there were only four nodes, formally called **Hosts.**
- In 1972, the **ARPANET** spread over the globe with 23 nodes located at different countries and thus became known as **Internet.**
- By the time, with invention of new technologies such as TCP/IP protocols, DNS, WWW, browsers, scripting

languages etc. Internet provided a medium to publish and access information over the web.

Advantages

Internet covers almost every aspect of life, one can think of. Here, we will discuss some of the advantages of Internet:

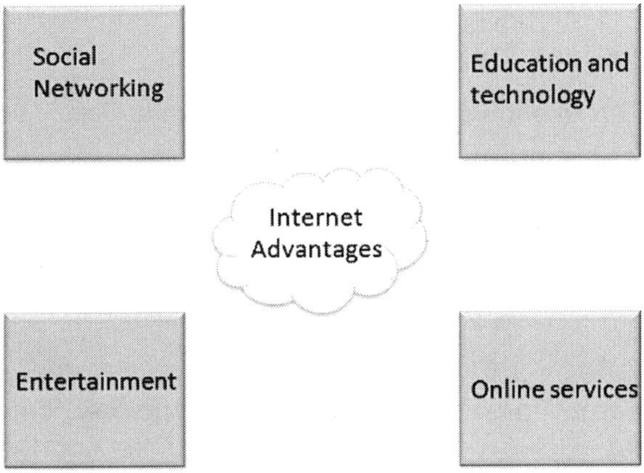

- Internet allows us to communicate with the people sitting at remote locations. There are various apps available on the wed that uses Internet as a medium for communication. One can find various social networking sites such as:
    - Facebook
    - Twitter
    - Yahoo
    - Google+
    - Flickr
    - Orkut
- One can surf for any kind of information over the internet. Information regarding various topics such as Technology, Health & Science, Social Studies, Geographical Information, Information Technology, Products etc can be surfed with help of a search engine.

- Apart from communication and source of information, internet also serves a medium for entertainment. Following are the various modes for entertainment over internet.
    - Online Television
    - Online Games
    - Songs
    - Videos
    - Social Networking Apps
- Internet allows us to use many services like:
    - Internet Banking
    - Matrimonial Services
    - Online Shopping
    - Online Bill Payment
    - Data Sharing
    - E-mail
- Internet provides concept of **electronic commerce**, that allows the business deals to be conducted on electronic systems

Disadvantages

However, Internet has proved to be a powerful source of information in almost every field, yet there exist many disadvantages discussed below:

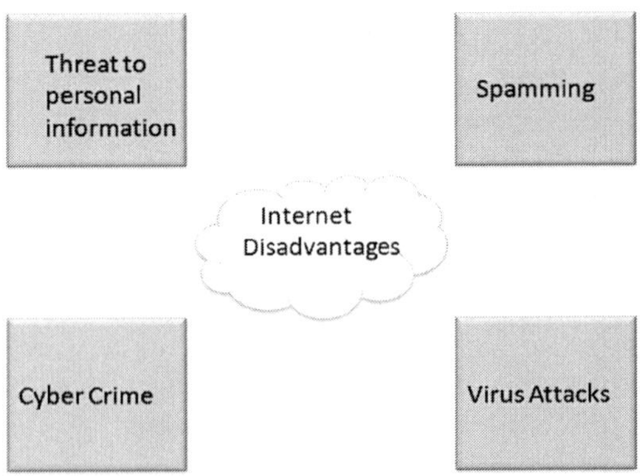

- There are always chances to loose personal information such as name, address, credit card number. Therefore, one should be very careful while sharing such information. One should use credit cards only through authenticated sites.
- Another disadvantage is the **Spamming**. Spamming corresponds to the unwanted e-mails in bulk. These e-mails serve no purpose and lead to obstruction of entire system.
- **Virus** can easily be spread to the computers connected to internet. Such virus attacks may cause your system to crash or your important data may get deleted.
- Also a biggest threat on internet is pornography. There are many pornographic sites that can be found, letting your children to use internet which indirectly affects the children healthy mental life.
- There are various websites that do not provide the authenticated information. This leads to misconception among many people.

Intranet

Intranet is defined as private network of computers within an organization with its own server and firewall. Moreover, we can define Intranet as:

- Intranet is system in which multiple PCs are networked to be connected to each other. PCs in intranet are not available to the world outside of the intranet.
- Usually each company or organization has their own Intranet network and members/employees of that company can access the computers in their intranet.
- Every computer in internet is identified by a unique IP address.
- Each computer in Intranet is also identified by a IP Address, which is unique among the computers in that Intranet.

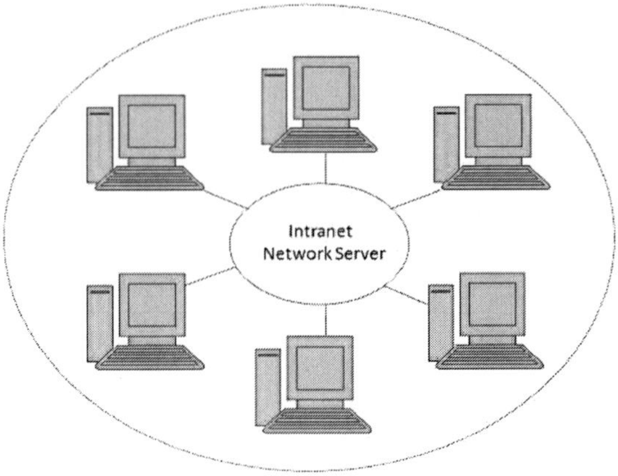

Benefits

Intranet is very efficient and reliable network system for any organization. It is beneficial in every aspect such as collaboration, cost-effectiveness, security, productivity and much more.

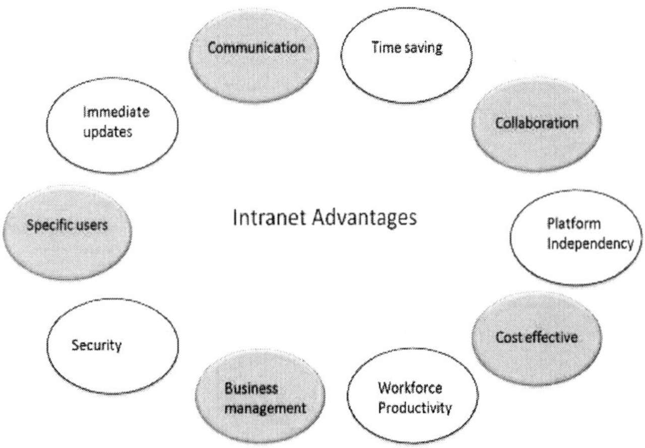

Communication

Intranet offers easy and cheap communication within an organization. Employees can communicate using chat, e-mail or blogs.

Time Saving

Information on Intranet is shared in real time.

Collaboration

Information is distributed among the employees as according to requirement and it can be accessed by the authorized users, resulting in enhanced teamwork.

Platform Independency

Intranet can connect computers and other devices with different architecture.

Cost Effective

Employees can see the data and other documents using browser rather than printing them and distributing duplicate copies among the employees, which certainly decreases the cost.

Workforce Productivity

Data is available at every time and can be accessed using company workstation. This helps the employees work faster.

Business Management

It is also possible to deploy applications that support business operations.

Security

Since information shared on intranet can only be accessed within an organization, therefore there is almost no chance of being theft.

Specific Users

Intranet targets only specific users within an organization therefore, once can exactly know whom he is interacting.

Issues

Apart from several benefits of Intranet, there also exist some issues. These issues are shown in the following diagram:

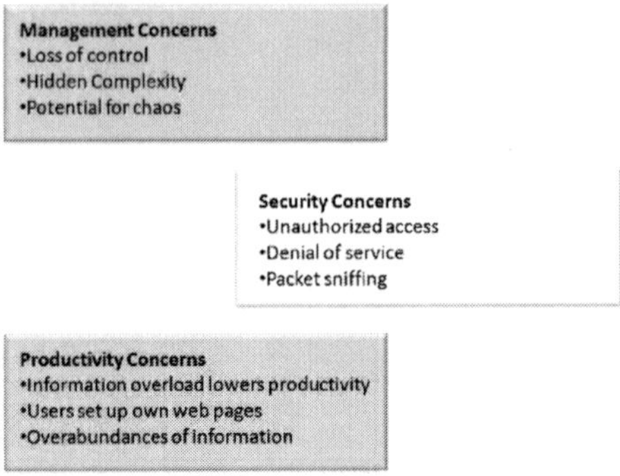

Applications

Intranet applications are same as that of Internet applications. Intranet applications are also accessed through a web browser. The only difference is that; Intranet applications reside on local server while Internet applications reside on remote server. Here, we've discussed some of these applications:

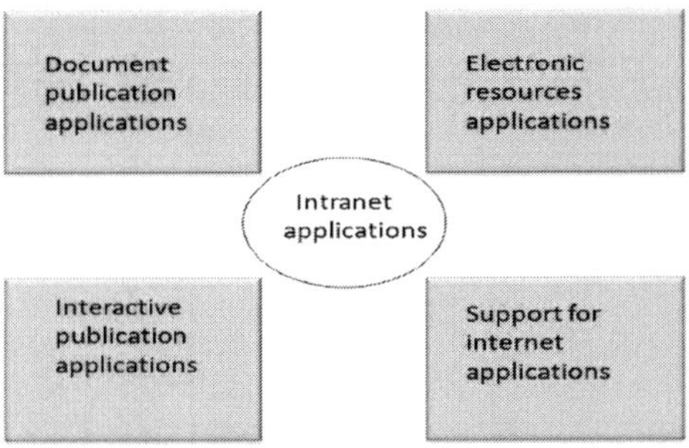

Document publication applications

Document publication applications allow publishing documents such as manuals, software guide, employee profits etc without use of paper.

Interactive Communication applications

Like on internet, we have e-mail and chat like applications for Intranet, hence offering an interactive communication among employees.

Support for Internet Applications

Intranet offers an environment to deploy and test applications before placing them on Internet.

Internet vs. Intranet

Apart from similarities there are some differences between the two. Following are the differences between Internet and Intranet:

Intranet	Internet
Localized Network.	Worldwide Network
Doesn't have access to Intranet	Have access to Internet.
More Expensive	Less Expensive
More Safe	Less Safe
More Reliability	Less Reliability

Email

Email is a service which allows us to send the message in electronic mode over the internet. It offers an efficient, inexpensive and real time mean of distributing information among people.

E-Mail Address

Each user of email is assigned a unique name for his email account. This name is known as E-mail address. Different users can send and receive messages according to the e-mail address.

E-mail is generally of the form username@domainname. For example, webmaster@starvetcol.ac.in is an e-mail address where webmaster is username and starvetcol.ac.in is domain name.

E-mail Message Components

E-mail message comprises of different components: E-mail Header, Greeting, Text, and Signature. These components are described in the following diagram:

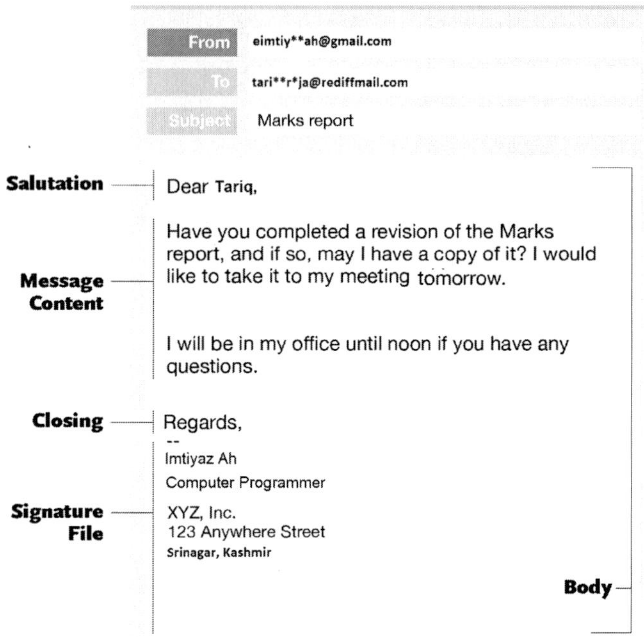

E-mail Header

The first five lines of an E-mail message is called E-mail header. The header part comprises of following fields:

- From
- Date
- To
- Subject
- CC
- BCC

FROM

The **from** field indicates the sender's address i.e. who sent the e-mail.

DATE

The **Date** field indicates the date when the e-mail was sent.

TO

The **To** field indicates the recipient's address i.e. to whom the e-mail is sent.

SUBJECT

The **Subject** field indicates the purpose of e-mail. It should be precise and to the point.

CC

CC stands for Carbon copy. It includes those recipient addresses whom we want to keep informed but not exactly the intended recipient.

BCC

BCC stands for Black Carbon Copy. It is used when we do not want one or more of the recipients to know that someone else was copied on the message.

GREETING

Greeting is the opening of the actual message. Eg. Hi Sir or Hi Guys etc.

TEXT

It represents the actual content of the message.

SIGNATURE

This is the final part of an e-mail message. It includes Name of Sender, Address, and Contact Number.

Advantages

E-mail has proved to be powerful and reliable medium of communication. Here are the benefits of **E-mail:**

- Reliable
- Convenience
- Speed
- Inexpensive
- Printable

- Global
- Generality

Disadvantages

Apart from several benefits of E-mail, there also exists some disadvantages as discussed below:

- Forgery
- Overload
- Misdirection
- Junk
- No response

Forgery

E-mail doesn't prevent from forgery, that is, someone impersonating the sender, since sender is usually not authenticated in any way.

Overload

Convenience of E-mail may result in a flood of mail.

Misdirection

It is possible that you may send e-mail to an unintended recipient.

Junk

Junk emails are undesirable and inappropriate emails. Junk emails are sometimes referred to as spam.

No Response

It may be frustrating when the recipient does not read the e-mail and respond on a regular basis.

Email Protocols

E-mail Protocols are set of rules that help the client to properly transmit the information to or from the mail server. we will discuss various protocols such as **SMTP, POP,** and **IMAP.**

SMPTP

SMTP stands for **Simple Mail Transfer Protocol.** It was first proposed in 1982. It is a standard protocol used for sending e-mail efficiently and reliably over the internet.

Key Points:

- SMTP is application level protocol.
- SMTP is connection oriented protocol.
- SMTP is text based protocol.
- It handles exchange of messages between e-mail servers over TCP/IP network.
- Apart from transferring e-mail, SMPT also provides notification regarding incoming mail.
- When you send e-mail, your e-mail client sends it to your e-mail server which further contacts the recipient mail server using SMTP client.
- These SMTP commands specify the sender's and receiver's e-mail address, along with the message to be send.
- The exchange of commands between servers is carried out without intervention of any user.
- In case, message cannot be delivered, an error report is sent to the sender which makes SMTP a reliable protocol.

SMTP Commands

The following table describes some of the SMTP commands:

S.N.	Command Description
1	**HELLO** This command initiates the SMTP conversation.
2	**EHELLO** This is an alternative command to initiate the conversation. ESMTP indicates that the sender server wants to use extended SMTP protocol.
3	**MAIL FROM** This indicates the sender's address.

S.N.	Command Description
4	**RCPT TO** It identifies the recipient of the mail. In order to deliver similar message to multiple users this command can be repeated multiple times.
5	**SIZE** This command let the server know the size of attached message in bytes.
6	**DATA** The **DATA** command signifies that a stream of data will follow. Here stream of data refers to the body of the message.
7	**QUIT** This commands is used to terminate the SMTP connection.
8	**VERFY** This command is used by the receiving server in order to verify whether the given username is valid or not.
9	**EXPN** It is same as VRFY, except it will list all the users name when it used with a distribution list.

IMAP

IMAP stands for **Internet Mail Access Protocol.** It was first proposed in 1986. There exist five versions of IMAP as follows:

1. Original IMAP
2. IMAP2
3. IMAP3
4. IMAP2bis
5. IMAP4

Key Points:

- IMAP allows the client program to manipulate the e-mail message on the server without downloading them on the local computer.
- The e-mail is hold and maintained by the remote server.
- It enables us to take any action such as downloading, delete the mail without reading the mail.It enables us to create, manipulate and delete remote message folders called mail boxes.

- IMAP enables the users to search the e-mails.
- It allows concurrent access to multiple mailboxes on multiple mail servers.

IMAP Commands

The following table describes some of the IMAP commands:

S.N.	Command Description
1	**IMAP_LOGIN** This command opens the connection.
2	**CAPABILITY** This command requests for listing the capabilities that the server supports.
3	**NOOP** This command is used as a periodic poll for new messages or message status updates during a period of inactivity.
4	**SELECT** This command helps to select a mailbox to access the messages.
5	**EXAMINE** It is same as SELECT command except no change to the mailbox is permitted.
6	**CREATE** It is used to create mailbox with a specified name.
7	**DELETE** It is used to permanently delete a mailbox with a given name.
8	**RENAME** It is used to change the name of a mailbox.
9	**LOGOUT** This command informs the server that client is done with the session. The server must send BYE untagged response before the OK response and then close the network connection.

POP

POP stands for Post Office Protocol. It is generally used to support a single client. There are several versions of POP but the POP 3 is the current standard.

Key Points

- POP is an application layer internet standard protocol.
- Since POP supports offline access to the messages, thus requires less internet usage time.
- POP does not allow search facility.
- In order to access the messaged, it is necessary to download them.
- It allows only one mailbox to be created on server.
- It is not suitable for accessing non mail data.
- POP commands are generally abbreviated into codes of three or four letters. Eg. STAT.

POP Commands

The following table describes some of the POP commands:

S.N.	Command Description	
1	**LOGIN** This command opens the connection.	
2	**STAT** It is used to display number of messages currently in the mailbox.	
3	**LIST** It is used to get the summary of messages where each message summary is shown.	
4	**RETR** This command helps to select a mailbox to access the messages.	
5	**DELE** It is used to delete a message.	
6	**RSET** It is used to reset the session to its initial state.	
7	**QUIT** It is used to log off the session.	
8	Mails once downloaded cannot be accessed from some other location.	Allows mails to be accessed from multiple locations.

S.N.	Command Description	
9	The e-mails are not downloaded automatically.	Users can view the headings and sender of e-mails and then decide to download.
10	POP requires less internet usage time.	IMAP requires more internet usage time.

E-mail System

E-mail system comprises of the following three components:

- Mailer
- Mail Server
- Mailbox

Mailer

It is also called **mail program, mail application** or **mail client.** It allows us to manage, read and compose e-mail.

Mail Server

The function of mail server is to receive, store and deliver the email. It is must for mail servers to be Running all the time because if it crashes or is down, email can be lost.

Mailboxes

Mailbox is generally a folder that contains emails and information about them.

Working of E-mail

Email working follows the client server approach. In this client is the mailer i.e. the mail application or mail program and server is a device that manages emails.

Following example will take you through the basic steps involved in sending and receiving emails and will give you a better understanding of working of email system:

- Suppose person A wants to send an email message to person B.
- Person A composes the messages using a mailer program i.e. mail client and then select Send option.

- The message is routed to **Simple Mail Transfer Protocol** to person B's mail server.
- The mail server stores the email message on disk in an area designated for person B.

The disk space area on mail server is called mail spool.

- Now, suppose person B is running a POP client and knows how to communicate with B's mail server.
- It will periodically poll the POP server to check if any new email has arrived for B. As in this case, person B has sent an email for person B, so email is forwarded over the network to B's PC. This is message is now stored on person B's PC.

The following diagram gives pictorial representation of the steps discussed above:

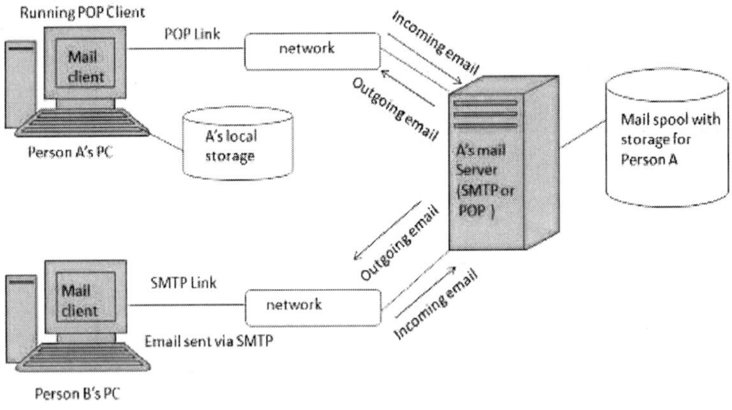